Where Fresh Waters Flow

The Restoration Plea

Cory Collins

CYPRESS

Copyright © 2025 by Cory Collins

Manufactured in the United States

Cataloging-in-Publication Data

Collins, Cory H. (Cory Hankins), 1955-

Where fresh waters flow: the restoration plea / Cory Collins.

rev. ed. p. cm.

Includes Scripture index.

ISBN: 978-1-956811-82-7 (pbk.); 978-1-956811-83-4 (ebook)

1. Churches of Christ—Doctrines. 2. Theology, Doctrinal. I. Author. II. Title.

230.663—dc20

Library of Congress Control Number: 2024948944

Cover design by Brittany Vander Maas.

For information:

Cypress Publications
3625 Helton Drive
PO Box HCU
Florence, AL 35630

www.hcu.edu

To my wife, Tanya, who has filled my heart, held my hand, and shown me my Lord for all these wonderful years. I would not be who I am without your love. I cannot count all the blessings God has given me through you. I love you more each day.

Contents

Foreword
Bill Bagents

I readily admit major positive bias toward the first edition (2007) of *Where Fresh Waters Flow*. Having worked with Cory Collins at Heritage Christian University, the Mars Hill Church of Christ, and in mission teaching on the Western Cape of South Africa, my experience with his skill, wisdom, and pleasantness is extensive. Those same excellent traits are also evident in his writing.

But *Where Fresh Waters Flow* neither needed nor desired a biased reading. The book stands on its merits. It presents the restoration plea from a biblical perspective in a compelling and engaging manner. The Bible is respected as the source of faith and religious authority. The reader is respected as being capable of both critical thinking and fair evaluation of evidence. There is no argumentation from emotion or mere tradition. The case for the principle of going back to God's revelation and intention is solidly documented. It reminds us that the return to fresh waters is essential to respect for God and submission to His will. That return is presented as a plea from God Himself.

And this revised (2025) edition of *Where Fresh Waters Flow* does more than preserve those admirable qualities; it enhances them. The new edition moves from 13 chapters to 20 with major expansion of content in the sphere of the biblical foundations of the principle of restoration. It offers additional details and examples without redundancy. While it's often true that less is more, that's not the case with this book. In this case, the "more" is clearer, stronger, and more compelling.

Besides the additional content, the revised edition also offers a strengthened emphasis—an even sharper focus—as each chapter flows directly from the "fresh waters" theme. God's fresh waters are pure, welcome, unpolluted, undiluted (undiluted in power, impact, authority), and unifying. God's fresh waters both guide and empower the never-ending (at least not this side of heaven), dynamic process of biblical restoration.

It could be argued that the revised edition doesn't lend itself as neatly to study in a single quarter within a Bible class curriculum. But I'd never have recommended limiting the 2007 version to a single quarter; the content was too rich and too important. Whether as part of a church's formal curriculum, an appeal to a friend to embrace God's truth more fully, family Bible study, or personal growth, *Where Fresh Waters Flow* offers blessings that should not be ignored.

Preface

When my friends and former colleagues at Heritage Christian University and Heritage Press invited me to write a revised edition of *Where Fresh Waters Flow*, I was delighted! Printed copies of the original 2007 book were becoming scarce, and they indicated that an updated version would be well received. They offered me the opportunity to revisit, revise, and expand that earlier publication. I'm so thankful that they did.

My family background and my life experiences have impressed upon me the importance of the Restoration Plea. My father, Ken Collins, was raised in a mainline Protestant denomination in Nashville, Tennessee. He met my mother, Mary Hankins, in Paris, Texas, during World War II. What an influence she had on him! He began to consider the Bible's teaching regarding the church Christ built and first-century Christianity.

As he heard and read God's Word, my father was convicted by its message. He repented of his sins, confessed Jesus Christ before others, and was baptized into Christ by immersion for the forgiveness of his sins. At that point, he became just a Christian, the same way that people became Christians back in the beginning.

Dad and Mom raised my brothers and me in that Christian faith, teaching and training us to follow Jesus. Dad became an adult Bible teacher and then served as an elder of the Hillsboro church in our hometown of Nashville for 28 years. He was an insurance agent, not a preacher in the typical sense. However, occasionally he would drive our family out of town to visit some small church where he would deliver the sermon.

In my adult life, the proposal to go back to the scriptures, back to "where fresh waters flow," has become more and more appealing. As I have studied and interacted with numerous people from various backgrounds and beliefs, I have sought to understand through church history the reasons behind various, conflicting views. I have also observed worsening religious divisions in my own generation. Such divisions are all so contrary to the unity for which Jesus prayed in John 17. It is shameful.

As I have written and as I now review this revised edition, I have several concerns. First, my intent in the book is to rebuild bridges back to God's inspired source, not erect more walls or strengthen preexisting walls between people and groups. One's goal must be to tear down walls, not add concrete to them! However, the bridge that must be restored is the bridge built on truth. The presentation of religious truth can be offensive to some, though such offense is not intended.

Second, the Bible talks about "speaking the truth in love" (Ephesians 4:15). God loves all people and therefore tells us the truth and expects us to follow it. In a similar way, I aim to love all people as I discuss God's truth. It is His truth and not my own. I want readers to know that I have tried to present His truth from a heart of love.

Third, I hope that any limitations or errors on my part will not get in the way of the book's overall principle. If my approach to this or that seems too narrow or too broad, too strict or too loose, let that not interfere with one simple fact. In order for Jesus's prayer to be answered positively and optimally, there must be unity among those who profess to follow Him. There is only one foundation or source for such unity. It is the pure, unadulterated Word of God.

Fourth, the addition of seven new chapters will not allow this revised edition to be studied in one thirteen-week series. In addition, the thirteen questions for thought and discussion at the close of each chapter may require more time per class session to cover fully. As a result, it may be helpful to spread the twenty chapters over a longer period, with more time allowed both for the material and the discussion involved. Or one may choose the chapters that seem most helpful and recommend the remaining material for further reading and study.

Finally, I pray that this book's resounding message will be, "Together, let's go back to the source, to the fresh waters of God's Word." The message is not, "Follow me" or, "Follow us." It is not, "Follow this great human reformer or reformation." It is rather, "Let us learn from the past, but return to the beginning, and let us know, worship, and serve the Lord as He has directed."

Any person, anywhere, at any time, may hear the gospel as presented in the New Testament, may respond to that gospel as the original recipients did, and may be added by the Lord to the same one church to which they belonged. No human being or group has a copyright or a patent when it comes to Christianity and the church. The church belongs to Christ and therefore may be called the church of Christ in addition to all the biblical other descriptors.

Efforts to return to God's fresh waters may be difficult

and messy at times. We may not always get everything right. We may not be able to remove every man-made element of division on a worldwide scale. However, it is worth all our effort to try. Let us seek to understand the will of God as given in scripture, to believe it, to obey it, and to teach it. That is the aim of this revised edition of *Where Fresh Waters Flow: The Restoration Plea*.

"[Jesus Christ] we preach, warning every man and teaching every man in all wisdom, that we may present every man perfect in Christ Jesus" (Colossians 1:28).

To God be the glory.

Cory Collins

January 2025

Chapter 1
Fresh Waters: The Idea
Psalm 63:1

W hen Tanya and I and our children lived in Nashville, Tennessee, we received a phone call one day from a man who offered to check the quality of the tap water in our house. We were interested because of course, we wanted to be assured that our water was safe and healthy. We made the appointment, feeling confident that someone from the city water utility company would come and check everything out.

We arranged for both of us to be home for the water test. The man came in, carrying a black box about the size of a briefcase. He opened it up, and we saw that it contained several vials or test tubes. With our permission, he poured water from our kitchen tap into a small, clear container. He said, "The water looks clear and pure, doesn't it?" We agreed, hoping that the water was just as clean as it appeared to be.

Then he said, "Now let me show you what's in your water that you *don't* see!" As he poured chemicals from his test tubes into the "pure" water, we saw very tiny things wiggling around near the bottom! The water wasn't as clean as it appeared to be. It was contaminated by various microorganisms that we had never seen before. It was not a pretty sight!

In fact, we had become so accustomed to drinking and using that tap water that we had never really questioned its purity. Could it be that we had been consuming all kinds of tiny pollutants that were now in our system? Had we swallowed some junk? Apparently so.

Then we had a second revelation on top of that one. Our earlier assumption that this water expert was from the utility company was wrong. He wasn't their representative at all. He was a salesman from a water softener company! He exposed the contaminants in our water so that he could then offer us his company's solution. He could sell and install a whole-house water softening system for "just" a few thousand dollars! So generous! So thoughtful!

There was a third eye-opener. The fellow's name was "Rusty!" We should have known! By the way, it turned out that our "contaminated" water was actually safe to drink. It met all the current health standards. In our opinion, Rusty had exaggerated the "problem" to create a need so that we would buy his product to address that need.

Fresh Water

God created us human beings with the capacity to become physically thirsty, and He created a world with the resources to quench and satisfy that thirst. In the very first chapter of the Bible, Genesis 1, the words "water" and "waters" together appear eleven times. Of course, the waters of the Flood meant both judgment upon the world and salvation for Noah and all that were in the ark (Genesis 6–8).

When Hagar, Sarai's maid, fled from Sarai, the angel of Yahweh (called in our English Bibles "the LORD") found her by a spring of fresh water and spoke with her there. That well was then called Beer-lahai-roi, which in Hebrew means, "the well of the Living One who sees me" (Genesis 16:7–14). Later,

Abraham sent away Hagar with their son Ishmael, and the water Abraham provided ran out. God opened Hagar's eyes and showed her a well (Genesis 21:14–19).

In fact, such wells were so precious because the lives of human beings and their flocks and herds could not survive for long without a regular supply of water. As a result, there was conflict between Abraham and the servants of Abimelech who had seized a well that Abraham had dug. As a result of their resolving the issue and taking an oath, that well was called Beersheba, which in Hebrew means "the well of the oath." Beersheba can also mean "the well of the seven," because Abraham gave Abimelech seven ewe lambs as a witness to show that he had dug the well (Genesis 21:22–34).

Of course, after the Exodus, the Israelites required water in the wilderness. On one occasion, after three days without water, when they were desperate, they came to water that was bitter. Therefore, the place was named Marah, which is Hebrew for "bitter." Yahweh showed Moses a tree, which Moses threw into the water so that it became sweet (Exodus 15:22–27). Then God led them to Elim, where there were no less than twelve springs of water.

At two different times and in two different locations, Yahweh twice provided the Israelites with thirst-quenching water from a rock (Exodus 17:1–7, Numbers 20:1–13). Wherever they were, it was as if the rock was "following" them, always available to satisfy their thirst. In the New Testament, Paul referred to this idea when he wrote to the Corinthians that the rock "followed" the Israelites in the wilderness. Paul went on to say, by inspiration, that "the rock was Christ" (1 Corinthians 10:4). In other words, just as the rock was always there for them, Christ is always there for His disciples who turn to Him in their thirst.

The Jews' annual seven-day Feast of Tabernacles (or Booths or Tents) (Leviticus 23:34; Deuteronomy 16:13, 16) also involved water. This feast commemorated the time of Israel's forty years of wandering in the wilderness, during which time they lived in tents and God supplied their food and water.

William MacDonald writes,

> Though not mentioned in the OT, the Jews had a ceremony of carrying water from the Pool of Siloam and pouring it into a silver basin by the altar of burnt offering for each of the first seven days of the Feast of Tabernacles. [1]

Craig S. Keener notes that "Pilgrims to the feast watched this ritual, which Jews throughout the Roman world thus knew about; it was even commemorated on souvenir jars they could take home with them."[2]

Fresh Life

In the Old Testament, physical thirst and refreshing water became a metaphor for man's deepest need for life and the Lord's singular ability to meet that need. The Old Testament clearly revealed that life without God at the center was stale, dry, and thirsty. Again and again, the people of Israel would turn to pagan gods like Baal and Asherah, or to the ways of the nations around them, or to possessions, pride, and power to satisfy their empty lives. Such vain pursuits continue today, with the same parched results.

Yahweh saved His people and gave them the Law that they might continue to enjoy His refreshing presence. Yet the Law itself could not provide true refreshment, because they chose to disobey His commands and thus only intensify their

1. William MacDonald, *Believer's Bible Commentary: Old and New Testaments*, ed. Arthur Farstad (Nashville: Thomas Nelson, 1995), 1512.
2. Craig S. Keener, *The IVP Bible Background Commentary: New Testament*, 2nd (Downers Grove, IL: IVP Academic, 2014), 271.

desperate condition. The Law certainly diagnosed their sinful ways and predicted the dire consequences that would result.

David and other psalmists wrote and sang about such thirst and their craving for God's thirst-quenching blessing. "As the deer pants for the water brooks, so my soul pants for You, O God. My soul thirsts for God, for the living God. When shall I come and appear before God?" (Psalm 42:1–2) "O God, You are my God; I shall seek You earnestly. My soul thirsts for You, my flesh yearns for You, in a dry and weary land where there is no water" (Psalm 63:1).

Repeatedly through the prophets, God promised to quench Israel's thirst, if only His people would turn to Him. Read, for example, Isaiah 41:17: "The poor and needy seek water, but there is none; their tongues fail for thirst. I, the LORD, will hear them; I, the God of Israel, will not forsake them." Also, see Isaiah 44:3: "For I will pour water on him who is thirsty, and floods on the dry ground; I will pour My Spirit on your descendants, and My blessing on your offspring."

Yahweh went on to offer through the prophet,

> Oh! Everyone who thirsts, come to the waters; and you who have no money come, buy and eat. Come, buy wine and milk without money and without cost. Why do you spend money for what is not bread, and your wages for what does not satisfy? Listen carefully to Me, and eat what is good, and delight yourself in abundance (Isaiah 55:1–2).

Fresh Choices

In the days of Jeremiah the prophet, the southern kingdom of Judah was on the brink of destruction and exile. In 586 BC Yahweh would send Nebuchadnezzar, the ruler of Babylon, to capture Jerusalem, burn the city, and take its citizens far away from their homeland.

These dire events would represent God's judgment upon His people. Why? They had chosen the wrong water, metaphorically speaking. Note His words through the prophet:

"Has a nation changed gods when they were not gods? But My people have changed their glory for that which does not profit. Be appalled, O heavens, at this, and shudder, be very desolate," declares the LORD. "For My people have committed two evils: they have forsaken Me, the fountain of living waters, to hew for themselves cisterns, broken cisterns that can hold no water" (Jeremiah 2:11–13).

"Have you not done this to yourself by your forsaking the LORD your God When He led you in the way? But now what are you doing on the road to Egypt, to drink the waters of the Nile? Or what are you doing on the road to Assyria, to drink the waters of the Euphrates? Your own wickedness will correct you, and your apostasies will reprove you; know therefore and see that it is evil and bitter for you to forsake the LORD your God, and the dread of Me is not in you," declares the Lord GOD of hosts (Jeremiah 2:17–19).

As a result, they would remain dry and thirsty.

Judah mourns and her gates languish; They sit on the ground in mourning, and the cry of Jerusalem has ascended. Their nobles have sent their servants for water; They have come to the cisterns and found no water. They have returned with their vessels empty; they have been put to shame and humiliated, and they cover their heads (Jeremiah 14:2–3).

What "fresh" choice should the Jews have made that would both please Yahweh and spare them from judgment? The answer is simple. They should have turned away from all other so-called sources of water and sought instead only the fountain of living water, Yahweh. By doing so, they would have found genuine refreshment and true life. Otherwise, they would surely have perished.

Such is the urgent need today of all who would seek to be faithful disciples who follow Jesus Christ. Let us reject the religious divisions, traditions, and creeds that have accumulated through the centuries. Let us recognize the contaminants and pollutants that have infiltrated the pure teaching of the Word of God. Let us go back "where fresh waters flow."

Questions for Thought and Discussion

1. What is the freshest, coldest, sweetest water that you have ever tasted?
2. Why don't we see all the contaminants that may be present in our water?
3. Why do we need a "Rusty" to help us identify them?
4. How significant is water in the Genesis account of creation?
5. How vital is water in sustaining all forms of life today?
6. Describe God's provision for Hagar in the wilderness.
7. How did God instruct Moses to turn bitter water into sweet?
8. Why would God choose water and thirst to illustrate spiritual truths?

9. Why would man reject God's living water for broken cisterns?
10. What happened to Jerusalem and Judah as a result?
11. Name some "broken cisterns" that people seek today but that cannot satisfy.
12. Can sincerity alone protect people of faith from becoming contaminated?
13. Is it necessary for all to return to the fresh waters of scripture? Is it possible?

Chapter 2
Fresh Waters: The Source
John 7:37–39

As indicated already, only the Word of God and the God of the Word can quench the thirst of the soul. The Old Testament prepared for the New by promising and prophesying that the Messiah (the Christ, literally the "Anointed One") would come. He alone would deliver the fresh water that would bring life and healing to a dry, parched world.

The Word of God, who was with God in the very beginning, and who Himself *was* God, would take on human form, become flesh, and reveal the essence and glory of God (John 1:1–18). John the Baptist identified Him as "the Lamb of God, who takes away the sin of the world" (John 1:29). Jesus came into a world that was stale, dry, and thirsty. Those who put their faith in Him enjoyed vibrant rejuvenation that the world could not supply and could not destroy. Local congregations were planted throughout the world, each one being an "oasis" where thirsty people could drink freely.

Therefore, any effort to seek and identify the fresh waters of early, authentic Christian faith and practice must begin with Jesus Christ Himself. His person, His message, His presence, and His power provide the only true source of what is genuine, pure, and real. He is the thirst quencher, and His words are the words of eternal life. Only He who first brought the living water from heaven can renew and restore the Christian and the church as we return to Him and follow His will.

John 4 records that a woman of Samaria came to Jacob's well at Sychar and that Jesus asked her for water.

> Then He said to her, "If you knew the gift of God, and who it is who says to you, 'Give Me a drink,' you would have asked Him, and He would have given you living water." ... "Everyone who drinks of this [physical] water will thirst again; but whoever drinks of the water that I will give him shall never thirst; but the water that I will give him will become in him a well of water springing up to eternal life" (John 4:10–14).

A well-known song says, "Jesus gave her water, and it was not from the well" (Anthony K. Music). Put yourself at that well and hear Jesus's words as He offered that woman—and He offers you—the water of life. You will want to bring your "village" to Jesus as she did (John 4).

In the previous chapter, we noted that the Old Testament prescribed the Jews' Feast of Tabernacles, which commemorated God's care and provision of food and water during their travels through the wilderness. The New Testament notes that Jesus Himself observed this feast, as John 7 indicates. Jesus used that occasion to make a remarkable promise. Note John 7:37–39:

> Now on the last day, the great day of the feast, Jesus stood and cried out, saying, "If anyone is thirsty, let him come to Me and drink. He who believes in Me, as the Scripture said, 'From his innermost being will flow rivers of living water.'" But this He spoke of the Spirit, whom those who believed in

Him were to receive; for the Spirit was not yet given, because Jesus was not yet glorified.

His Ministry

After His baptism and His temptations, Jesus began His ministry by declaring the coming arrival of something fresh, new, exciting, and radical, the kingdom of heaven! As Isaiah had predicted over 700 years earlier (Isaiah 9:1–2), Jesus entered Galilee and brought heaven's light into the world's darkness (Matthew 4:12–16). His first recorded words were, "Repent, for the kingdom of heaven is at hand." God would rule the hearts and lives of men and women who would repent of sin and come to enjoy the privilege of submission and surrender to Him.

Then He called the four fishermen, Peter, Andrew, James, and John. He taught in the Jewish synagogues, proclaiming the gospel (good news) of the kingdom, and healing the sick and demonized. People came from far away. Large crowds followed Him because He was the source of fresh water, bringing hope, peace, joy, and healing.

His Message

Next, Jesus went up on a hillside, sat down, and delivered what is known as the Sermon on the Mount (Matthew 5–7). Take a personal, in-depth tour of that sermon. Go with Jesus to that spot in your mind, focus your attention on His words, and open your heart to believe. Read the sermon aloud at one sitting or have someone else read it while you listen. Let Jesus's words sink in afresh.

Think of the paradoxical qualities of a blessed, happy life, typically called the Beatitudes (Matthew 5:3–12). Consider the disciples' influence as compared to salt and light.

Hear Jesus speak with authority as He sets the record straight regarding what is right in God's sight (Matthew 5:21–48). Reflect on His teaching regarding religious acts like giving, prayer, and fasting (Matthew 6:1–18). Focus on His answer to matters related to money, anxiety, and priorities (Matthew 6:19–34). Recognize the danger of a critical spirit and the beautiful clarity and simplicity of treating others as you would want to be treated (Matthew 7:1–12).

Follow through to the sermon's conclusion as Jesus describes the either-or decision you must make about following Him (Matthew 7:13–27). Choose the narrow road that leads to life. Build on the rock foundation presented in the sermon, determining to put Jesus's teachings into practice. Be awestruck by His authority (Matthew 7:28–29). Come away refreshed and renewed.

His Offer

No wonder Jesus described the new birth as requiring both the physical element (water) and the divine agent (the Holy Spirit). He told Nicodemus in John 3:3–5,

> "Most assuredly, I say to you, unless one is born again, he cannot see the kingdom of God." Nicodemus said to Him, "How can a man be born when he is old? Can he enter a second time into his mother's womb and be born?" Jesus answered, "Most assuredly, I say to you, unless one is born of water and the Spirit, he cannot enter the kingdom of God."

The fact that Jesus intended actual physical water (baptism) here as the element of the new birth is evident from the context in John. According to John 3:22, Jesus and His disciples came into the land of Judea, and "there [Jesus] remained with them and baptized." John 4:1 adds that "Jesus made and baptized more disciples than John (though Jesus Himself did not baptize, but His disciples)." In this case, He used the real, earthly item (water) and infused it with the spiritual significance of the beginning of a new life.

His Encounters

Jesus elsewhere described the fresh newness He would provide in this way, in Luke 5:36–38:

> No one puts a piece from a new garment on an old one; otherwise, the new makes a tear, and also the piece that was taken out of the new does not match the old. And no one puts new wine into old wineskins; or else the new wine will burst the wineskins and be spilled, and the wineskins will be ruined. But new wine must be put into new wineskins, and both are preserved.

The scribes and Pharisees, hard, dry, and brittle like old wineskins, could not accept the fresh "wine" of Jesus's teaching. They would reject and resist His message rather than stretching to receive it and benefit from it. Such old, unchangeable "wineskins" would be destroyed.

Deciding to drink of Jesus's fresh water means recognizing one's past hardness and sinful ways. It means yielding in humble, obedient faith, opening one's heart and life so that the nourishing fountain of Jesus Christ might flow into it.

Watch Jesus enter Simon Peter's boat and then experience the abundant catch of fish that was caught in the breaking nets. Hear Peter declare his sinfulness and hear Jesus say, "Do not fear! From now on you will be catching men!" It is no surprise that these fishermen left everything and followed Jesus (Luke 5:1–11).

Imagine yourself as the paralytic, unable to walk but

lowered on a mat through a hole in the roof to meet Jesus. Hear Him say, "Son, your sins are forgiven you." And then, "I say to you, arise, take up your bed, and go to your house." How could you help but arise, take up your bed, and go out in the presence of others as he did? It is no wonder that, when he did so, all were amazed and glorified God, saying, "We never saw anything like this!" (Mark 2:1–12)

Visit the home of Simon the Pharisee and watch Jesus's interaction with him and with the sinful woman who entered and washed His feet with her tears (Luke 7:36–50).

Sit on the road to Jericho with Bartimaeus, the blind beggar. Feel the thrill of having your sight restored. You will want to jump up and run after Jesus down the road as he did (Mark 10:46–52). How could you not?

Go with Mary Magdalene and the other Mary to Jesus's tomb. There has been an earthquake. An angel from heaven has rolled the stone away. That angel has told you to go quickly to tell His disciples that He has risen. Those women ran; so would you! (Matthew 28:1–8)

His Renewal

That challenge also applies to you and me if we have become dry and stale after our conversion. Do you lack the fire and the passion that you first experienced after your conversion? Do you remember the first time you met Jesus as you learned of Him from the inspired gospels, you genuinely repented of your sins, you confessed His sweet name, and you were clothed with Him in baptism? Oh, the joy, peace, and relief of that moment! And then the "honeymoon" began, as you started to learn to walk with Him. The more effectively you can relive and revisit that initial thrill of knowing Jesus Christ, the more successfully you can be refreshed again and again.

Without proper care, anything that is once fresh can become dry, dead, and stale. Most often it is personal sin that makes the freshness of meeting Jesus Christ stale. The spirit becomes burdened and weary. The joy of scriptural meditation, prayer, singing, and evangelism becomes stagnant. Can it be reclaimed? Can the thirst be renewed and quenched once again? Yes indeed! Freshness is renewed by radical repentance. As Peter told the crowd in Acts 3:19 after the healing of the crippled beggar, "Repent therefore and be converted, that your sins may be blotted out, so that times of refreshing may come from the presence of the Lord."

The need for renewal also applies to the church universal and to each congregation. Jesus called the church in Ephesus, which had left its first love, to remember, repent, and return (Revelation 2:4–5). Later we read, "The Spirit and the bride say, 'Come.' And let the one who hears say, 'Come.' And let the one who is thirsty come; let the one who wishes take the water of life without cost" (Revelation 22:17). Returning to Jesus, the source of fresh waters, is the key to restoring the identity, faith, and practice of the church Christ came to build.

Questions for Thought and Discussion

1. How would you describe the woman at the well in John 4? Her daily routine?
2. Why wasn't physical water sufficient to refresh her heart and her soul?
3. How did her immoral life choices prevent the quenching of her thirst?
4. Why are some people more aware of their spiritual thirst than others?

5. How does unconfessed sin, rather than quenching one's thirst, leave one dry and stale?
6. What "artificial drinks" does the world offer, that never truly satisfy?
7. How might thirsty people deny, minimize, or mask their spiritual needs?
8. Why would a person turn to alcohol, drugs, immorality, or money to quench his or her thirst?
9. Why do some people find social media, smartphones, and the Internet so satisfying?
10. How does the devil or the world persuade people to keep pursuing such "water?"
11. What do you find refreshing about the life, ministry, and teaching of Jesus Christ?
12. Why are there so many churches? What do some use, besides the gospel, to attract people?
13. How can you recognize substitute "thirst quenchers" offered in the name of religion?

Chapter 3
Fresh Waters: The Content
John 6:63

We have considered the fact that human beings require water, both physical and spiritual, to survive and thrive. We have seen that the only genuine, reliable source of water is the true and living God, who has spoken in His word. That God-given word provides the only content of fresh, living water. With that in mind, we now note what the Bible itself emphasizes regarding the God-given origin and authority of its message.

In the Beginning

When God created the heavens and the earth, He spoke the universe into existence with nothing but His eternal word. Some ten times Genesis 1 declares, "And God said ... and it was so." Whether it was light or the firmament or the division of waters and land or vegetation or the sun, moon, and stars or fish and fowl or beasts and creeping things or man and woman, it was the power of God's word that made it happen. God said it, and it happened.

Yahweh placed man and woman in a beautiful garden in

Eden. From Eden, a river flowed to water the garden, and from there it parted and became four riverheads (Genesis 2:10). Two of these four were the Tigris and Euphrates (Genesis 2:14). The land was fertile and lush because it was supplied by fresh water. All was well with Adam, Eve, and God in that initial period.

What was the first question recorded in the Bible? Who raised that question, and what was being questioned? The first question was, "Has God indeed said, 'You shall not eat of every tree of the garden'?" It was the cunning serpent asking the first woman, Eve. He taunted her regarding Yahweh's prohibition of the fruit of the tree of the knowledge of good and evil. In other words, it was the authority of the word of God that was challenged, more specifically the single word, "not."

By rejecting the content of God's truth and choosing instead the serpent's lie, Eve and then her husband Adam ate the forbidden fruit, bringing sin, death, and spiritual drought upon the earth. The consequences of their decision were dire, simply because they refused to heed one particular word that Yahweh had spoken, the word "not." They were expelled from Eden, and they could no longer drink from the source of fresh water that flowed from it. What a powerful metaphor.

Of course, water and the word of God were connected again in the universal flood that occurred in the days of Noah (Genesis 6–9). The water that Yahweh had created to nourish life He then used to extinguish life, because the world at that time had rejected His authoritative word.

One may study Genesis and see this principle on every page. Whether it was God's promises to Abraham or His destruction of Sodom and Gomorrah for their homosexual immorality, His word was the last word—the only word that mattered. When He commanded Abraham to offer Isaac and then stopped him from doing so, it was the word of God that carried full authority. He blessed Jacob and changed his name to Israel, swearing to make him a great nation.

Yahweh gave Joseph dreams of his coming rule over his brothers and his parents. He sent dreams also to the butler and the baker, who were fellow prisoners with Joseph in Egypt. Pharaoh himself received two parallel dreams regarding the coming years of plenty and then of famine. Before Joseph died God restated through him the promise of the coming exodus.

In each and every case, whatever God said happened. Each person was free to heed the divine message and live or to reject it and die, but no one could overturn or negate the word of God. Speaking figuratively, whether one's thirst was quenched or whether one's life was deserted and dry depended on just one thing. That one thing was one's relationship to the fresh water that springs only from the mouth of God. So it was then, and so it is now.

In Old Testament Law

In the book of Exodus, one sees the conflict between the word of Pharaoh and the word of Yahweh. The one commanded that newborn Hebrew males be put to death, the other that they be allowed to live. Not fearing the Egyptian king's edict, Moses's mother protected him so that he eventually became Israel's deliverer. Then Yahweh's ten plagues against Egypt, her king, and her gods made clear the authority of His word over all others. At Mount Sinai, God's voice thundered from heaven as He issued the Ten Commandments and His other laws. The people could accept or reject His covenant, but they could not alter it. The tabernacle for worship was to be built "according to the pattern which you were shown" (Exodus 26:30). There was to be no deviation.

Throughout the Pentateuch, the first five books of the

Bible that contain the Law of Moses, examples abound
regarding the absolute, exclusive, unique authority of the
word of God. There were specific instructions for every sacrifice and every other item connected to worship. There were
rules for the priests and Levites, as well as directions for the
three annual feasts. There were clear moral boundaries,
dietary restrictions, and so much more.

That first generation coming out of Egypt perished
because of their disobedience to God's word. In the book of
Deuteronomy, Moses urged the next generation to remember
what had happened, to obey the Lord, and to teach their children, lest they face the same end. He said:

> You shall not add to the word which I command you, nor
> take from it, that you may keep the commandments of the
> LORD your God which I command you (Deuteronomy
> 4:2).

> Only take heed to yourself, and diligently keep yourself, lest
> you forget the things your eyes have seen, and lest they
> depart from your heart all the days of your life. And teach
> them to your children and your grandchildren ...
> (Deuteronomy 4:9).

> Therefore, you shall be careful to do as the LORD your God
> has commanded you; you shall not turn aside to the right
> hand or to the left. You shall walk in all the ways which the
> LORD your God has commanded you, that you may live and
> that it may be well with you, and that you may prolong your
> days in the land which you shall possess (Deuteronomy 5:32–
> 33).

Before Moses died, he warned the Israelites of their future
disobedience and punishment. He said to them:

Set your hearts on all the words which I testify among you today, which you shall command your children to be careful to observe—all the words of this law. For it is not a futile thing for you, because it is your life, and by this word you shall prolong your days in the land which you cross over the Jordan to possess (Deuteronomy 32:46–47).

In Old Testament History, Poetry, and Prophecy

When Joshua succeeded Moses as Israel's leader, Yahweh told him clearly:

... observe to do according to all the law which Moses My servant commanded you; do not turn from it to the right hand or to the left, that you may prosper wherever you go. This Book of the Law shall not depart from your mouth, but you shall meditate in it day and night ... For then you will make your way prosperous, and then you will have good success (Joshua 1:7–9).

Before he died, Joshua challenged those who would outlive him by repeating what God had said to him. "Therefore, be very courageous to keep and to do all that is written in the Book of the Law of Moses, lest you turn aside from it to the right hand or to the left ..." (Joshua 23:6).

In the Book of Judges, God's people fell away from His life-giving word within just one generation (Judges 2:7–10). The result was chaos, as the Hebrews were attacked and oppressed again and again, for years at a time. By sharp contrast, the contemporary Book of Ruth showed the peace, harmony, and prosperity that resulted when God's word was obeyed.

Space will not permit further detailed illustrations in Old Testament history of this simple principle, that the word of

God was and is the only source of fresh, life-giving, nourishing water. One could consider Samuel (1 Samuel 3:1–10) on
the positive side or King Saul on the negative (1 Samuel 13:1–
15, 15:1–35). In fact, one may pick any king, any at all, and see
the outcome that resulted either from obedience or
disobedience.

Ultimately, Israel's disobedience and idolatry resulted in
the exile of the northern kingdom in 722 BC. Judah followed
suit, fell to Babylon in 586 BC, and suffered in exile for 70
years. Only when the people repented and again sought God's
fresh waters did He bring them home again.

In biblical poetry, particularly the Book of Psalms, God is
praised for his word. Read Psalm 19, which celebrates the
world of God and the *word* of God. Consider Psalm 119, in
which each of its 176 verses affirms the unique value of God's
statutes, laws, precepts, and testimonies.

The biblical prophets, moved by the inspiring Spirit of
God (2 Peter 1:20–21), consistently preached the word of God
as the only standard and source of ultimate truth. They called
their contemporaries to believe, repent, and obey. They
promised that their God-breathed words (2 Timothy 3:16–17)
would be fulfilled, ultimately by the coming Messiah. As
Isaiah wrote, "The grass withers, the flower fades, but the
word of our God stands forever" (Isaiah 40:8).

In the Teaching of Jesus Christ and the New Testament

The New Testament claims that all scripture is God-breathed
(2 Timothy 3:16–17). The New fulfills the Old and builds upon
its foundation. It asserts that Jesus's virgin birth, for example,
fulfilled "that which was spoken by the Lord through the
prophet" (Matthew 1:22–23).

In the words of Jesus Himself, "For assuredly, I say to you,
till heaven and earth pass away, one jot or one tittle will by no

means pass from the law till all is fulfilled" (Matthew 5:18). The "jot" was the *yodh,* the smallest letter in the Hebrew alphabet. The "tittle" was any tiny stroke or projection in a Hebrew letter that distinguished it from any similar letter that lacked such a tittle.

Jesus also said, when He predicted the fall of Jerusalem within one generation, "Heaven and earth will pass away, but My words will by no means pass away" (Matthew 24:35). After His resurrection, He spoke of the things written concerning Him in the Law of Moses, the Prophets, and the Psalms (Luke 24:25–27, 44–48).

Jesus also promised the apostles that the Holy Spirit would speak in them so that they would convey His words (Matthew 10:19–20). With God's word, they would bind and loose that which God had bound or loosed already in heaven (Matthew 16:19, 18:18). The Spirit would teach them all things, bring to their remembrance all that Jesus had said, and guide them into all truth (John 14:26, 16:13–15). The Spirit would come upon them on the Day of Pentecost (Acts 1–2).

Therefore, the New Testament documents, though given through men during that first-century apostolic period, would originate with the Holy Spirit (Galatians 1:1–2). They would carry divine authority as inspired Scripture (1 Thessalonians 2:13, 2 Peter 3:14–18). As a result, in conclusion, it is in scripture alone that one finds the fresh waters that lead, feed, and nourish men and women in our relationship with God. It is to scripture alone that we must turn and cling, recognizing and resisting any and all efforts to dilute it, deny it, add to it, or take from it.

Questions for Thought and Discussion

1. Describe the significance of the phrase "And God said" in the Genesis creation account.
2. Could man have survived without the fresh, life-giving water that God provided in Eden?
3. God defined marriage as the union of one man and one woman. How is that challenged today?
4. To tempt Eve to sin, the serpent had to discredit God's Word. How does that happen today?
5. How did the Flood reveal the invincible power of God's Word regarding judgment?
6. What did God promise Abram and Sarai, that seemed impossible at the time?
7. Why did God declare that He would destroy Sodom and Gomorrah (and then do it)?
8. What do the events in Exodus (plagues, the Red Sea, or Mt. Sinai) indicate about God's Word?
9. What did Moses repeatedly say about obedience and disobedience in Deuteronomy?
10. Give other Old Testament examples of the authoritative content of God's Word.
11. How did Jesus affirm the truth, accuracy, and authority of the scriptures?
12. What did Jesus say about the truth of God's Word as the apostles would present it?
13. Why must we affirm the inspired scriptures as the only pure source of fresh waters?

Chapter 4
Fresh Waters: The Issue
Acts 20:28–31

From the dawn of time man has chosen either to compromise, contaminate, or cast aside the only true water of life, described in the Spirit-breathed Word of God. Sometimes people polluted it by adding unauthorized ingredients. Sometimes they limited it by disregarding its elements or reducing its potency. Sometimes they abandoned it entirely and substituted some appealing alternative. In any and every case, the result was the same. God's people cut themselves off from His thirst-quenching presence and became dehydrated. They needed a restoration, a return to where fresh waters flow. Learning from the past, one can come to understand the present.

The Past

Previously we noted as examples Adam and Eve, Noah's generation, the era of the Judges, and the kings of Israel. We could cite multiplied cases that illustrate the same truth. One could either obey the Word of God and live or defy the Word of God and die.

Think about Aaron's sons, Nadab and Abihu, who offered strange (unauthorized) fire on God's altar, "which He had not commanded them" (Leviticus 10:1). So, "... fire came out from the presence of the LORD and consumed them, and they died before the LORD" (verse 2).

Consider the days of King David, when unauthorized people (non-Levites) transported the ark of the covenant in an unauthorized way, on a cart drawn by oxen. As a result, when the oxen stumbled, one of the drivers named Uzza did something else unauthorized. He reached out his hand to steady the ark. 1 Chronicles 13:10 records, "The anger of the LORD burned against Uzza, so He struck him down because he put out his hand to the ark; and he died there before God."

David corrected the arrangement before trying again! Note the following from 1 Chronicles 15:2, 13, and 15.

> Then David said, "No one is to carry the ark of God but the Levites; for the LORD chose them to carry the ark of God and to minister to Him forever." ... "Because you did not carry it at the first, the LORD our God made an outburst on us, for we did not seek Him according to the ordinance." ... The sons of the Levites carried the ark of God on their shoulders with the poles thereon, as Moses had commanded according to the word of the LORD.

David's son Solomon multiplied wives for himself, directly disobeying God's explicit prohibition (Deuteronomy 17:17). As God had said, those wives turned Solomon's heart away after other gods. Therefore, Yahweh promised to tear the kingdom from him, which He did in the days of Solomon's son, Rehoboam (1 Kings 11:1–13).

All of these cases, and too many more to mention here, reveal how man has often responded disobediently to God's plan. They also show the consequences of those responses. Finally, they demonstrate the solution, humbly and penitently restoring man's faith and practice to conform with God's design. Having seen this throughout the Old Testament, we can more clearly understand what has happened since Jesus Christ first established His church.

The Pattern

After Simon Peter confessed Jesus to be the Christ, the Son of the living God (Matthew 16:16), Jesus declared: "You are Peter, and on this rock I will build My church" (Matthew 16:18). Making a play on words with Peter's name (Greek, *petros,* a stone), Jesus promised to build His church on no mere stone but rather on solid bedrock (Greek, *petra*). It is true that Peter and the other apostles would surely be authorized to bind and loose what was previously bound and loosed in heaven (Matthew 16:19, 18:18). However, they would do so as representatives of Jesus Christ. The church would certainly not be built on any mortal man, not even Peter. Jesus clearly exposed his fallibility moments later, when Peter denied that Jesus would go to the cross and when Jesus therefore rebuked him with the words, "Get behind Me, Satan!" (Matthew 16:22–23)

The scripture confirms that Christ Himself, whom Peter confessed, would be the foundation on which the church was based. 1 Corinthians 3:11 reads, "For no man can lay a foundation other than the one which is laid, which is Jesus Christ." 1 Peter 2:6–8 identifies Jesus as the precious cornerstone, quoting Isaiah 28:16, Psalm 118:22, and Isaiah 8:14.

In contrast with today's thousands of denominational churches and community churches, Jesus Christ spoke of only one church. It was in fact not just non-denominational, but pre-denominational. He called it "My church." When we today speak of Jesus's church, the Lord's church, or the church of Christ, we simply seek to honor Jesus's own identification of the single, original church that He established. The church as He described it belongs to Him and not to any man, board, government, minister, or pastor.

Let that sink in. There is a prevailing common assumption that various kinds of churches, with differing creeds, traditions, and practices, are pleasing to God or at least acceptable to Him. However, the Bible teaches that the very idea of a divided "Christianity" is repulsive to God! The night before He died, Jesus Himself prayed regarding His future followers, "that they may all be one; even as You, Father, are in Me and I in You, that they also may be in Us, so that the world may believe that You sent Me" (John 17:21).

Jesus Christ is not only the sole foundation and sole owner of His one church. He is the only head of that one body, and He is its singular Savior as well. Jesus Christ, who died on the cross for the sins of the world, is the central focus of Scripture, the central focus of the church, and the central focus of this study. This series considers the church's faith and practice out of gratitude to Christ, whose grace and authority the church must reflect. We dare not separate the doctrine of the church from the person and work of Christ, for they are inextricably joined as one.

The Lord's one church began in Jerusalem, on the first Jewish Day of Pentecost after Jesus's resurrection, likely in AD 30 or AD 33. Filled with the Holy Spirit, Peter and the other apostles were enabled to preach in various languages. They proclaimed that Jesus of Nazareth had been accredited by God, crucified by man, and raised from the dead as predicted a thousand years earlier by King David. He was confirmed beyond a doubt as Lord and Christ (Acts 2:22–36).

On that day about 3,000 people heard the message and responded to it in repentance and baptism. They were then added together by the Lord, becoming the first church or congregation of Christians (Acts 2:37–47). All the apostles and early believers were part of this one body, with Jesus Christ as the one Head. Their unity was rooted in one Spirit, one hope, one Lord, one faith, one baptism, and one God (Ephesians 4:4–6).

This one church was composed of many local congregations. The *people* were imperfect, but the *pattern* of God's Word was perfect (2 Timothy 1:13–14, Philippians 3:17). The apostles used this divine pattern to instruct and correct the churches (1 Corinthians 4:17, 7:17, 14:34–37; Revelation 2–3). They taught others who were to teach still others the same unchanging message (2 Timothy 2:2). Jesus made this point by saying, "Teach them to observe all that I commanded you" (Matthew 28:20).

The Problem

When Jesus prayed for the unity of all His future followers, He also prayed, "Sanctify them in the truth; Your word is truth" (John 17:17). However, in defiance of His prayer, men did what they had done from the days of Adam and Eve. They distorted and polluted God's fresh water.

Paul told the elders from Ephesus: "From your own number men will arise and distort the truth in order to draw away disciples after them. So be on your guard!" (Acts 20:30–31) The apostles often predicted that false teachers would introduce error and corrupt the church, and that sincere people would follow them and be lost. They anticipated false doctrines, distortions of scripture, and departures from the faith. Note 1 Timothy 4:1–16; 2 Peter 2:1–3, 3:14–18; 1 John 2:18–19; Revelation 2:14–16, 20–23. The Holy Spirit guided the apostles to write the various New Testament letters for the express purposes of preventing and correcting such deviations.

About AD 125 a new office of "bishop" developed. Rather than a plural group of men overseeing one local church as the Scriptures indicate (Acts 14:23), this one bishop ruled a diocese (a group of congregations). After AD 150 these bishops formed councils that convened, made new rules, and imposed them on the individual dioceses and churches.

When Constantine made "Christianity" the official religion of the Roman Empire in the 4th century, pagan citizens and soldiers with various beliefs came into the church. Heathen feasts were renamed and welcomed as Christian holy days and festivals such as Christmas. Idolatry gave way to the adoration of images of saints, martyrs, and the Virgin Mary.

Augustine in the 4th century proposed the doctrine of original sin, the idea that infants are born with the guilt of Adam and Eve. From this belief came the need for infant baptism (for the forgiveness of this inherited sin) and eventually sprinkling as an alternative to immersion. There also arose the doctrine of the Immaculate Conception, the idea that the Virgin Mary was conceived without original sin, so that she would not "pass it on" to her infant son Jesus. Limbo was proposed as a place between Heaven and Hell where non-baptized infants go when they die.

As the official Roman church became more worldly, some retreated to seek a more spiritual life as monks in monasteries and nuns in convents. Also during this time, church leaders were required to leave their wives and children and become celibate or else be removed from their roles.

The church's organization came to parallel that of the Roman Empire in a pyramid-style structure. Presiding bishops, later called patriarchs, emerged in five key cities: Alexandria, Antioch, Constantinople, Jerusalem, and Rome. After many contests, the Roman bishop took the title of "papa-father" or "pope" and became the spiritual equivalent of the Roman emperor.

The church claimed that the church had always had a pope, beginning with the apostle Peter. However, Peter did not meet the criterion of celibacy (Mark 1:30), nor was he regarded as the earthly head of the church (Galatians 2:11–14).

As the Roman Empire declined, the Roman pope claimed political power over nations and kings. As such he would be the head of both church and state, intertwined and inseparable.

Many more new, nonbiblical teachings emerged. These include papal infallibility, the assumption of Mary into heaven, purgatory between heaven and hell, the redefinition of "saints," prayers to Mary and saints, making the sign of the cross, the seven sacraments, transubstantiation (the miraculous change of the bread and wine into Christ's actual flesh and blood), confession of sin to priests, the sale of indulgences, the veneration of icons and relics, the hierarchy of archbishops and cardinals, the praying of the rosary, the creation of canonical law, and more.

These innovations became possible because the authority of the Bible was compromised, contaminated, and cast aside. As a result, thirsty people began to yearn for God's fresh waters.

Questions for Thought and Discussion

1. How does the case of Nadab and Abihu show the dangers of changing God's "fresh waters"?
2. Read 1 Samuel 13:8–12. How and why did King Saul go beyond God's authorized plan?
3. Since God never prohibited moving the ark on a cart, how could that have been wrong?

4. How did Solomon pollute God's "fresh waters," and with what result?

5. Read 1 Kings 12:25–33. How and why did King Jeroboam change worship in Israel?

6. Explain how Jesus used Peter's name to make a play on words regarding the church.

7. Since Jesus called it "My church," is it biblical to describe it as "the church of Jesus Christ"?

8. When Jesus used the singular term "church," did He intend multiple, divided denominations?

9. When did that one church of Christ begin? What was preached that day?

10. How did some 3,000 souls respond that day and why? To what church were they added?

11. What pivotal change in church leadership and authority occurred around AD 125 and AD 150?

12. How did Augustine's promotion of "original sin" lead to further pollution of "fresh waters"?

13. How did the papacy develop, and what other new church teachings and practices were created?

Chapter 5
Fresh Waters: The Precedents
Revelation 2:5

Yahweh told the prophet Zechariah to proclaim, "Return to Me, and I will return to you" (Zechariah 1:3). Though the developing Roman church declined further and further into apostasy, there would come calls for reform and restoration, a return to where fresh waters flow.

As the developing Roman church became increasingly centralized and institutionalized, the magisterium (the church's teaching authority) continued to decree various man-made traditions and practices. The pope was said to be infallible when speaking *ex cathedra* (Latin for "from the chair"). Not having the Bible in their own languages, people were dependent upon what their priests told them, either from the Bible or from tradition. The worship service, called the "mass" (from the Latin word for dismissal), was recited in a foreign tongue.

Before there would be significant efforts to return where fresh waters flow by restoring the church of Jesus Christ, there would be further difficulties and divisions. Just as we have seen in the Bible itself, men continued to move farther and farther into spiritual drought. As Yahweh had spoken through the prophet Jeremiah centuries earlier,

> "Be astonished, O heavens, at this, and be horribly afraid; Be very desolate," says the LORD. "For My people have committed two evils: They have forsaken Me, the fountain of living waters, and hewn themselves cisterns—broken cisterns that can hold no water" (Jeremiah 2:12, 13).

The East-West Schism—AD 1054

We mentioned previously the conflict and competition among the five patriarchs, including one in Rome and another in Constantinople. After a period of growing estrangement between the two, the Eastern churches (led by the patriarch of Constantinople, Michael Cerularius) and the Western church (led by Pope Leo IX) mutually excommunicated each other in AD 1054. Serious differences, both political and theological, led to this ultimate separation.

The Eastern and Western leaders disagreed over the universal rule of the pope, which the East rejected. They held conflicting views regarding the nature of the procession of the Holy Spirit, the use of leavened versus unleavened bread for the Eucharist (the Lord's Supper), the use of religious icons (pictures) versus statues ("graven images"), and more. The West required that leaders be celibate; the East required that they be married. The Eastern churches kept their singing a cappella (without man-made instruments), and they immersed newborn infants three times (once in the name of the Father, then in the name of the Son, and third in the name of the Holy Spirit). They rejected sprinkling. We could list additional distinctions between the two.

The Western church became known as Roman Catholic, with catholic meaning "universal" or "as a whole." The

Eastern churches were identified as Eastern Orthodox, with orthodox meaning "straight thinking" or "correct doctrine." In their respective countries, they were called Greek Orthodox, Russian Orthodox, etc.

The Western Schism—AD 1378-1417

The Western church divided further. From 1378 to 1417, in the Roman Catholic Church, when there were two, and later three, simultaneous rival popes. Each pope had his own following, his own Sacred College of Cardinals, and his own administrative offices. Each pope excommunicated the two other popes and insisted that he was the legitimate "Holy Father," the visible, earthly head of the worldwide ("catholic") church.[1]

From 1309–1377, the popes took up residence in Avignon, France, rather than Rome, due to current political conditions.

> After Pope Gregory XI reestablished the papal capital in Rome in 1377, cardinals of the Sacred College selected a second pope, who assumed the vacant Avignon seat. There was a succession of such "antipopes," and the schism was not healed until 1417. The increased power and ambitions of the cardinals had led, no doubt, to the schism and the subsequent emergence of conciliarism, a theory that a general council of the church has greater authority than the pope and may, if necessary, depose him.[2]

Again, much more detail could be given.

---

1. https://www.britannica.com/event/Western-Schism
2. https://www.britannica.com/event/Avignon-papacy

Cries for Reform

Numerous individuals arose in reaction to these religious divisions and man-made doctrines, seeking to correct biblically the errors they saw in the increasingly apostate church. They sounded the alarm, calling for a return to the faith and practice of the original church. Long before Thomas Campbell, Alexander Campbell, Barton W. Stone, Walter Scott, and others, there were those who sought, if not a full restoration, at least significant steps in that direction.

For example, consider Peter Waldo (c. AD 1140–c. 1205), a wealthy clothing merchant in Lyons, France. Waldo sold his possessions and used the proceeds to give the Bible to the people in their own tongue. He had translations made from the Latin New Testament. This was much earlier than Gutenberg's printing press, which was not invented until AD 1440. He formed an order of evangelists who gained many followers in central and southern France, called Waldenses or Waldensians. They sold their possessions and lived lives of poverty. Their lifestyle was a striking contrast to the wealth, worldliness, and laxity of the established church and its leaders.

They used various slogans, such as, "Everyone ought to believe, for the gospel has spoken." "Scripture speaks, and we ought to believe." "Whatever is not enjoined in Scripture must be rejected." "The Bible is the only safe guide in religion." They called for the church to return to the pure teaching of Scripture. They rejected masses and prayers for the dead. They denied purgatory as unbiblical. They defended "lay (non-clergy) preaching." They believed that they could preach the Word of God without the permission or approval of the Catholic Church. They preached with a missionary emphasis, in the local language, with a strong New Testament emphasis.

They rejected the intermediary role of the clergy. They

rejected all Catholic feast-days, festivals, and prayers, with a couple of exceptions. They refused to take oaths, since they said the Bible prohibited such. Around AD 1181, the Archbishop of Lyons prohibited their scriptural preaching. The Waldensians responded by preaching even more zealously. They were violently opposed and bitterly persecuted by the Roman Catholic Church. In AD 1184 at Verona, Pope Lucius III excommunicated the Waldensians and other similar groups. He directed that they should be eliminated by church inquisition and secular punishment.

They were driven from France to hide in the valleys of northern Italy. They organized the movement as a church with bishops, priests, and deacons. They began to claim to be the "true" church. In AD 1214 Pope Innocent described the Waldensians as heretics and schismatics.[3]

As a second example, note John Wycliffe in England (AD 1300–1384). A priest in the Catholic Church, he was considered to be the ablest theologian at Oxford University. He taught, "The scriptures are the only law of the church." "Scripture is the property of the people." He said that no papal decree was valid unless it was consistent with the scriptures. He asserted that in the original church, there were only two classes of officers—elders and deacons. He declared that God spoke to men only through the Bible and not church leaders and councils.

Wycliffe called out the Pope for his avarice, tyranny, and usurping of power and privilege. He said church leaders should be, like Peter, without silver or gold (cf. Acts 3:6). He called the pope "antichrist." He said the claims of the papacy

---

3. *Eerdmans Handbook to the History of Christianity*, 315–317.

were unhistorical and that the moral unworthiness of priests invalidated their office and sacraments.[4]

Long after his death, the Council of Constance declared Wycliffe a heretic on May 4, 1415. His works were to be burned and his bodily remains removed from consecrated church ground. This order, confirmed by Pope Martin V, was eventually carried out in 1428. Wycliffe's remains were dug up and burned, and the ashes were thrown into the River Swift.

The Reformation Movement continued to grow. Martin Luther (1483–1546) was a German Catholic priest and monk. In 1517, he first protested to the Catholic church about the sale of indulgences (payment for the full or partial remission of temporal punishment for sins). He argued that only faith in Christ, and not money or meritorious works, could forgive sins. Luther posted ninety-five theses, criticizing church practices, on the door of the Castle Church of Wittenberg.

He was excommunicated in 1520 for refusing to recant. Condemned as an outlaw, he went into hiding. During that time, he translated the Bible into German. Luther begged his followers not to call themselves Lutherans, but only Christians, based on Paul's words in 1 Corinthians 1:12–13. Though seeking to reform the church, Luther continued infant sprinkling and other Catholic traditions. He denigrated the book of James as "an epistle of straw."[5]

John Calvin (1509–1564) also rebelled against the Catholic sacramental system, man-made tradition, and man-centered works of merit to gain salvation. He insisted that even man's response to the gospel was predetermined and produced by God, who had sovereignly chosen whom to save. Calvin

---

4. Herring, George, *Introduction to the History of Christianity* (New York: New York University Press, 2006), 230.

5. *Luther's Works*, vol. 35, *Word and Sacrament I* (Philadelphia: Fortress, 1960), 395–97.

falsely taught that those God had not selected were unable to have true faith and receive salvation.

The Anabaptists (meaning "re-baptizers") also emerged, in Switzerland, in the 1500s. They rejected infant baptism and insisted on believers' baptism instead. They were therefore persecuted by both the Catholics and the Protestants. Their movement was called the "Radical Reformation."

We could add John Huss (1373–1415), Jerome Savanarola (1452–1498), Ulrich Zwingli (1484–1531), William Tyndale, (1494–1536) John Knox (1505–1572), Robert Sandemann (1718–1771), John Wesley (1703–1791), and many others.

In spite of their efforts at reform, these men and movements resulted in Protestant denominations. They often wore the names of their founders, documented their beliefs, and required strict adherence to them. They wrote their own distinctive creeds and manuals, and they chose their own nonbiblical names. They splintered, split, and divided still further. All of today's denominations trace back to the doctrines and practices of these men. The result was not a restored church defined by the New Testament pattern, but rather a confusing plethora of conflicting leaders, beliefs, ideas, and practices. And yet, God's fresh waters were still available!

Questions for Thought and Discussion

1. How did the developing Roman church move even farther away from God's fresh waters?
2. What factors led to the East-West Schism of AD 1054?
3. What were the two resulting denominations called, and what were their differences?

4. How did their primary distinction—the question of authority —contribute to their division?
5. What further controversy arose in the West from AD 1378–1417?
6. What do you find commendable about Peter Waldo's character, beliefs, and leadership?
7. What happened to John Wycliffe's body after his death, because he had defied Rome?
8. Why would Martin Luther have prohibited the use of the term "Lutherans?"
9. What did the Anabaptists teach that provoked both the Catholics and Protestants?
10. Why didn't these reform efforts result in a united, biblical church of Jesus Christ?
11. Research any modern denomination. What are its origins and distinctive beliefs?
12. What can you find about the history and beliefs of a state church, like the Church of England or the Church of Scotland?
13. Research the beliefs and worship practices of any "non-denominational" community church.

Chapter 6
Fresh Waters: The Plea
1 Corinthians 1:10–13

The Restoration Momentum

Though well intentioned, over time the movements begun by the Protestant Reformers led to further divisions. Man-made names, creeds, and practices grew. Denominations formed in order to crystallize and formalize the teachings and interpretations of fallible, mortal men. Parts of the Bible were preached, but only as they had been explained by the founders of these new churches.

For example, "Calvinism" referred to the theological system proposed by John Calvin. Another name for that system was "Reformed Theology." The doctrines of total depravity, unconditional election, limited atonement, irresistible grace, and the perseverance of the saints reflected the conclusions that Calvin reached. Scriptures that contradicted his views were minimized or with great effort forced to fit into his system. Calvin wrote the *Institutes of the Christian Religion* in AD 1536, in which he interpreted and sometimes overruled Scripture.

For instance, Calvin made himself an authority regarding the mode of baptism. He wrote,

> Whether the person baptized is to be wholly immersed, and that whether once or thrice, or whether he is only to be sprinkled with water, is not of the least consequence: churches should be at liberty to adopt either according to the diversity of climates, although it is evident that the term *baptize* means to immerse, and that this was the form used by the primitive Church.[1]

It seems ironic that Calvin while rebelling against the human authority and tradition of the Catholics, would claim such authority for himself. While acknowledging that immersion was the New Testament mode of baptism, yet, he himself simply asserted that the mode was irrelevant. If one was "of Calvin" (see 1 Corinthians 1:12), he or she might accept Calvin's words as authoritative, though they contradicted what he himself had said that the Word of God authorized!

In a similar way, "Lutheranism" formulated the religious perspectives of Martin Luther, and "Wesleyanism" developed according to what John Wesley had believed and taught. The Mennonites came along, wearing the name of Menno Simons. The Amish followed Jacob Amman, a Mennonite himself who sought to reform the Mennonite movement.

Some new denominations arose, named after forms of church government. "Presbyterian" referred to churches being led by groups of elders, while "Episcopalian" was a term used of churches led by bishops. Some groups took the names of specific doctrines. "Baptist," for example, referred to various denominations that practiced only baptism by immersion.

---

1. John Calvin and Henry Beveridge, *Institutes of the Christian Religion*, vol. 3 (Edinburgh: The Calvin Translation Society, 1845), 344.

"Methodism" had to do with the "methods" of teaching employed by John and Charles Wesley.

These groups eventually divided among themselves, sometimes geographically. The "Southern" denominations (Southern Baptists, Methodists, and Presbyterians) and the "Northern" groups separated due to matters related to the Civil War. Other splits occurred over doctrinal matters, such as differences over man's free will or the inerrancy and inspiration of the scriptures.

Ironically, man-made confessions and creeds were written by the very people who rejected man-made confessions and creeds (of the Catholic Church)! For example, one who wanted to preach for a Presbyterian church would have to "subscribe to" (promise to uphold in every way) the Westminster Confession of Faith rather than, or in addition to, the Bible alone. Because the various Protestant groups differed significantly over matters such as baptism, conversion, worship, and church government, they became separate "fellowships" with multiple, contradictory "faiths." They left the one body, one faith, one Lord, and one baptism foundation described in Ephesians 4:1–6. They failed to maintain "the unity of the Spirit in the bond of peace." Many who saw all this were convicted by a simple yet profound idea: return to God's original plan.

The Restoration Movement

In the late 1700s and the early 1800s Thomas Campbell, Alexander Campbell, Barton W. Stone, Walter Scott, and many others saw the sectarian, denomination ruptures among those who professed to follow Christ. They dreamed of turning back the clock, peeling back the accumulated layers of man-made names, creeds, councils, and divisions. They realized that anyone in modern times could hear and believe the original gospel message preached in the beginning and recorded in the New Testament. If such a person responded as believers were taught to respond in the first century, they would receive the same salvation and become what they were —Christians.

These "restorers" called for a return to the simple faith and practice of the New Testament. Their goal was neither to form yet another denomination nor to create an ecumenical "union" of all the denominations, but rather to recapture the identity of the first-century church that began in Jerusalem on the Day of Pentecost in AD 33 (or possibly AD 30).

In fact, they could preach exactly what Peter and the other apostles preached on that day, as recorded in Acts 2. That message focused on Jesus Christ: His accreditation by His miraculous deeds, His crucifixion due to God's plan and man's sin, His resurrection from death, His appearances to eyewitnesses, and His ascension to the Father's right hand. He had miraculously poured out the Holy Spirit, so that each one present could hear the gospel in his or her own tongue. God had clearly made this Jesus, the one whom the people had crucified, both Lord and Christ.

Pricked to the heart, those in the crowd asked, "What shall we do?" Following the apostles' instructions, some three thousand repented of their sins and were immersed that same day so that their sins would be forgiven. They received the gift of the Holy Spirit, and as a result they were added together to Christ and, therefore, the church.

The apostles and converts all belonged to the same church! There was no other. It was not a Catholic Church, as that church would later develop. Neither was it a Protestant church, founded and started by Reformers in the 1500s. It was just the church, plain and simple. It was established by Christ, bought by His blood, and subject to Him as the one head of that one body. It could be described as the church of

God, the churches of Christ, the Way, the household of faith, etc. These terms were descriptive and not sectarian or denominational. Its members were Christians, saints, or disciples—not Catholics, Baptists, Methodists, Lutherans, Presbyterians, etc.

So, these restorers determined to preach and practice what that original church did. They left their various denominational affiliations, names, and creeds. Those who had not done so were baptized as penitent believers by immersion for the forgiveness of their sins. They aimed to do Bible things in Bible ways and call Bible things by Bible names. They evaluated religious beliefs in the light of Scripture, determined to accept and teach only what they found there. They refused to add to the Word of God, to take away from it, or to make substitutions for it.

They discovered nothing "new" that others had not seen before. Rather, they *rediscovered* clear biblical teaching that had been there all along. Some of that doctrine had been forgotten, minimized, overruled, or rejected.

Based on this restoration conviction, they came to practice baptism only by immersion, and only for believers (not infants). They observed the Lord's Supper on the first day of every week. They appointed elders, deacons, and evangelists to lead and serve the local churches. They recognized the autonomous or independent nature of each congregation. They refused to establish a hierarchy or earthly headquarters. They used the Old Testament for instruction, but they understood that only the New Testament prescribed the specific elements of the church's worship and practice. They taught that the Holy Spirit worked through the preaching of the gospel to convert sinners to Christ. They preached that, to respond to the grace of God, one must hear the gospel, believe the gospel, confess Jesus as the Son of God, repent of sin, and be baptized. They claimed that one could thus become a Christian and be added by the Lord to the same original church described in the New Testament, without ever joining any human denomination.

Church division and denominationalism violated the commands of God (1 Corinthians 1:10). Therefore, these churches of Christ (Matthew 16:18, Romans 16:16) appealed for all believers in Christ to abandon all denominational divisions, to unite upon Scripture alone, and to follow the New Testament pattern given to the early church. Their aim would be, "In matters of faith, unity. In matters of opinion, liberty. In all things, charity (love)."

A Restoration Perspective

In this study, it is vital that we keep these key principles in mind:

1. Jesus Christ and the cross are the center and heart of everything related to the church. Jesus Christ *is* the doctrine of the church (1 Corinthians 2:2), and every doctrine or practice is for His glory. Clearly one is not to worship the Bible, the church, or its faith and practices; one worships the Christ to whom the Bible and the church's faith and practices point.

2. Some vital biblical teachings are not restoration issues because they are not disputed. The two great commands are still to love God and to love one's neighbor (Mark 12:28–32). Christ's death, burial, resurrection, and appearances are still "of first importance" (1 Corinthians 15:1–8. Attitudes such as humility, patience, compassion, and generosity must never be minimized.

3. This discussion is not intended to question the faith, love, or sincerity of any person who is trying to follow Christ. Rather, the aim is to evaluate various teachings and practices objectively, to see if they conform to the clear teaching of the Word of God. We must be allowed to question various religious teachings without being judged as arrogant or "holier than thou."

4. The question is not, "Who is right?" but rather, "What is right?" It's not, "What does 'your church' believe about X?" but rather, "What does the Bible teach about X?" Nothing is right or wrong just because of any religious group's view of it.

5. External forms (such as the mode of baptism or the frequency of the Lord's Supper) must not be separated from their internal function and meaning. It is possible, but wrong, to get all the forms right while not engaging the heart in genuine repentance and adoration. We must not!

6. No human being or group owns the Restoration Plea. As noted, churches of Christ seek to align with the first-century church. However, anyone, anywhere, at any time, may hear the gospel, respond to it biblically, and be added to the same one church described in the New Testament. The plea is non-denominational and non-sectarian.

7. Some may point to perceived failures or flaws in the attempt by churches of Christ to restore the church. They may see apparent inconsistencies or weaknesses. However, the plea itself is still valid, and all are encouraged to pursue restoration afresh in every generation.

Questions for Thought and Discussion

1. How does John Calvin's teaching about baptism illustrate the causes of religious division?
2. How did the names and beliefs of some of today's denominations develop?
3. To what church did all the apostles and first-century converts belong?
4. If people respond to the gospel as taught in Acts 2, to which church are they added?
5. Could such persons assemble and humbly say, "We are part of the Lord's church"?
6. Why would they not be "Stoneites," "Campbellites," "Scottites," etc.?
7. How does the Bible prohibit denominational divisions in 1 Corinthians 1:10–13?
8. Do churches of Christ seek their origin in the 19th century or in the first century?
9. Do these churches offer a "better denomination" or a return to "no denomination"?
10. How can such churches wear Christ's name biblically without becoming a denomination?
11. How can such Christians invite others to abandon man-made names and creeds?
12. How is the Restoration Plea centered on Jesus Christ and Him crucified?
13. Paraphrase each of the seven key principles noted at the end of this chapter.

Chapter 7
Fresh Waters: the Alternatives
2 Timothy 4:1–6

O n March 29, 2024, the Gallup organization asked, "How Religious Are Americans?"[1] The report noted,

> According to an average of all 2023 Gallup polling, about three in four Americans said they identify with a specific religious faith. By far the largest proportion, 68%, identify with a Christian religion, including 33% who are Protestant, 22% Catholic and 13% who identify with another Christian religion or simply as a "Christian."
>
> Seven percent identify with a non-Christian religion, including 2% who are Jewish, 1% Muslim and 1% Buddhist, among others.
>
> Twenty-two percent of Americans said they have no religious preference, and 3% did not answer the question.

Of course, Gallup used the word "Christian" culturally, to refer to anyone who professes to follow Christ. Yet here is a simple, undeniable fact. Religious confusion and division are

---

1. https://news.gallup.com/poll/358364/religious-americans.aspx.

inseparably tied to one basic issue: religious authority. If you asked anyone, "What do you believe religiously, and why?" that person would inevitably point to his or her primary religious authority.

Virtually all answers to all religious questions depend on one's answer to this fundamental question: "What is the source of religious authority?" Unless all parties in a conversation can agree on that question, they will never come to unity on the issues that divide them.

For example, imagine that you and I decide to coach two teams as they compete against each other in baseball. You believe that there should be three bases plus home plate, that each half-inning should consist of three outs, and that each team must have nine players at any one time. You have been reading the official manual! However, imagine that I propose one more base, two more outs, and three more players per team. I am passionate about this, and I refuse to budge, because this is the way my beloved grandfather played when he was a boy.

You will never make any progress with me, even though you are right, because we cannot agree on the source of authority. If you challenge my baseball rules, I may object by asking, "Are you saying that my grandfather was wrong and that he did not play by the rules? He was sincere! He was devoted! The players on his team loved him!"

Now imagine that we invite a third coach to tell us what he believes. He has yet another set of rules, based on his family, his favorite teacher, his personal feelings, the majority views of other people, etc. What will result? There will be three separate baseball "denominations," each following a different set of regulations and interpretations!

So, what are some other sources of religious authority, besides just taking the Bible alone, that influence the beliefs and practices of people today? There are sure to be more than the ones we list here, but we can certainly make a solid start. It is not our intent to be unkind, harsh, disrespectful, or arrogant. We love and respect each person who reads what follows, and we only ask that each reader consider these matters as objectively as possible. It's not personal!

Church Tradition

We have previously discussed the development of councils, creeds, and dogmas that have become additional sources of authority for Catholic and Protestant denominations. Some believe that the Catholic Church was the original church, that therefore the apostles were Catholics, and that therefore the Catholic Church produced the Bible. Therefore, the church preceded the New Testament and has authority over it. They say that Jesus gave the keys of authority to Peter, who passed that key down through a succession of popes, who then may speak with divine authority regarding doctrines previously unknown. They claim that the Bible need not authorize praying to the saints and to Mary, for example, because the church has done so.

Of course, such an approach inevitably leads to ever-changing rules. With each new pope, there may be a hardening, or more likely a softening, of matters relating to faith, fellowship, and morality. For example, read Wikipedia's discussion of the Vatican II Ecumenical Council of 1962–1965.[2] Also research, for instance, contrasting statements made by Pope Francis and previous popes regarding homosexuality and same-sex unions.[3]

Among mainline Protestants, consider the major changes

---

2. https://en.wikipedia.org/wiki/Second_Vatican_Council.

3. https://www.npr.org/sections/thetwo-way/2013/07/29/206622682/pope-francis-discusses-gay-catholics-who-am-i-to-judge.

in the moral teachings of the United Methodist Church, as noted in revisions of their authoritative *Book of Discipline*. In May 2024, The General Conference voted by an overwhelming majority to remove the language that the "practice of homosexuality ... is incompatible with Christian teaching."[4] Yet this was clearly a statement that the General Conference had previously *approved*, based on the Scriptures (e.g., 1 Corinthians 6:9–11).

When Jesus taught regarding man-made traditions, Jesus quoted God's word through Isaiah: "And in vain they worship Me, teaching as doctrines the commandments of men" (Matthew 15:9).

Continuing Revelation

Some find their religious authority in additional visions, prophecies, charismatic leaders, and cults. While typically recognizing the Bible as one source of authority, they believe that the Holy Spirit continues to reveal authoritative, God-given messages beyond the Bible. However, the Bible itself indicates that the days of such inspiration have passed.

Until the New Testament was completed, while prophecy and revealed knowledge were still partial (1 Corinthians 13:9), the Holy Spirit provided the church with special gifts of miracles and revelation. Then, when prophecy and revealed knowledge would be perfected and completed, those supernatural gifts would be done away and would end (1 Corinthians 13:10). The biblical canon (authoritative scripture) would be closed at that point, with nothing to be added or changed.

The Pentecostal and Charismatic movements, however, insist that revelation continues today through ecstatic

---

4. https://www.wnccumc.org/understanding-general-conference-2024-faqs.

tongues-speaking, dreams, and visions. Oddly, they do not add their newly-revealed information to the Bible, though they insist that the same Holy Spirit has given them this information. In addition, these individuals and groups contradict each other in their beliefs and practices, showing that in fact they do not have a united, Spirit-given message.

The Church of Jesus Christ of Latter-Day Saints, known as the Mormons, teach that an angel named Moroni led Joseph Smith in 1830 to translate the Book of Mormon. They hold this book to be of equal authority with the Bible, but purer, since they claim that parts of the Bible have been lost or corrupted. Though they say that the 1830 original edition was perfectly translated word for word, church leaders have revised that "inspired" edition with thousands of changes.[5] The Mormons teach that miracles, prophecies, and revelations continue through their President and the Twelve Apostles. They teach that God the Father has "a tangible body of flesh and bones" (but see John 4:23–24) and that all human beings pre-existed in heaven as spirits."[6] Numerous groups have spun off of the Mormons. One of these is the Community of Christ, formerly called the Reorganized Church of Jesus Christ of Latter-Day Saints, which adheres to the original, unedited, 1830 edition of the Book of Mormon.[7]

Other Alternatives

Subjective emotions: Many will say: "If it *feels* right, it must *be* right! I know I am saved because I feel it. Whatever the Bible says or does not say, I know what is in my heart."

---

5. http://www.utlm.org/onlinebooks/3913intro.htm.

6. https://www.churchofjesuschrist.org/study/manual/new-testament-semi nary-teacher-manual/appendix/basic-doctrines?lang=eng.

7. https://en.wikipedia.org/wiki/List_of_churches_in_the_Latter_Day_Saint _Reorganization_movement.

Some will assuredly claim, "God told me ..." and dare others to question them. The Bible warns us that what merely *seems* right may lead to death rather than life (Proverbs 14:12).

Persuasive preachers: A powerful magician named Simon once wowed people so that they called him "the great power of God" (Acts 8:10)! Billy Graham, and today his son Franklin Graham, have convinced many that they are saved without baptism into Christ (Romans 6:1–4). Books such as the *(Popular Preacher) Study Bible* sell widely. Joel Osteen, Max Lucado, Beth Moore, and other "dynamic," "passionate" speakers have influenced many.

Itching ears: People are consumers, and they may shop for churches, or even hop churches, looking for what they want. The prophets noted long ago that their peers loved to hear pleasant messages of peace, prosperity, and comfort (Jeremiah 5:31, Micah 2:11). Paul exhorted Timothy to preach the word. He foretold that Christians would want to have their ears tickled. They would accumulate to themselves teachers according to their own desires (2 Timothy 4:1–5).

Family ties: When precious, loving parents or grandparents were sincerely in error regarding biblical teaching, family members hesitate to "betray" them by following scripture. Yet, Jesus spoke of the possible family cost of obeying Him (Matthew 10:35, Luke 14:25–35). My own father left his own Protestant family roots to respond to the gospel in repentance and baptism.

Cultural norms: It has always been easier to fit in than to stand out. The broad way is popular, and Jesus said that most would choose to go with the crowd. However, only the minority path, which He called strait (tight or difficult) and narrow, leads to life (Matthew 7:13–14). To those who seek convenience, Jesus says, "Deny yourself and take up the cross" (Luke 9:23).

Financial gain: The Bible warns frequently and

strongly against the love of money (1 Timothy 6:9–11). Church overseers must be free from the love of money (1 Timothy 3:3). The Old Testament seer Balaam loved the wages of unrighteousness (2 Peter 2:15–16). Some may "choose a church" based on their desire to further their careers financially.

Latest trends: Like the people of ancient Athens (Acts 17:21), many today spend their time either telling or hearing some new thing. The gospel may seem to them boring, outdated, or unappealing. They focus more on being relevant and engaging than on being biblical and challenging. Subjects like sin, repentance, death, and hell are just not attractive to them.

We close this chapter with a severe warning. "But even if we, or an angel from heaven, preach any other gospel to you than what we have preached to you, let him be accursed ... For do I now persuade men, or God? Or do I seek to please men?" (Galatians 1:8, 10)

Questions for Thought and Discussion

1. What do Gallup polls and your own observations indicate about religion today?
2. What single question is a primary key to all questions about religious differences?
3. Why can it be difficult to discuss these matters objectively without causing offense?
4. What are some dangers of church traditions, whether Catholic, Protestant, or other?
5. Groups that claim continuing, Spirit-given revelation teach contradictory things. Why?
6. If the original Book of Mormon was inspired, why were large parts of it later deleted?

7. How do you see people basing their beliefs on feelings rather than fact?

8. While study Bibles can be of some help, why should we be cautious with them?

9. One "itching-ear" promise today is health, wealth, and prosperity. Discuss.

10. Describe how and why Saul of Tarsus (Paul) and others left family ties for Jesus.

11. How does popular culture pressure followers of Jesus to conform?

12. What negative impact can money have on church leaders and organizations?

13. What current fads and trends are used to draw people to various kinds of churches today?

Chapter 8
Fresh Waters: Direct Statements
John 4:24

W e began our study using an analogy with water. We noted that fresh water, springing from its source, is healthy, pure, and nourishing. Yet, as it travels downward, it can easily become stale, contaminated, polluted, and even stagnant. Try as we might, it is extremely difficult to "fix" the affected water by "reforming" it and removing all its additives. However, we can "start fresh" by returning to the beginning, "where fresh waters flow." We used that as a picture of our approach to the restoration of the one church of the Bible, the church of Jesus Christ. Rather than try to repair Catholic or Protestant churches, our plea is to return to God's initial plan for His church. We aim to be objective in our quest and to treat all people with respect and kindness.

But How?

All this raises the question, just *how* do the Scriptures authorize? How can we recognize His fresh waters and cling to them? How can we identify contaminants and avoid introducing them as others have? How can we be Christians, disciples, saints, brothers and sisters in the one church, without aligning ourselves with the various denominational groups that have developed? How can we stay away from the entertainment focus, the fads, and the people-pleasing approaches that are so popular today? How can we know for certain what God requires, allows, and prohibits?

Because God in the Bible accommodated Himself to address His creatures in ways that we can understand, He used avenues of authority that are common to us in everyday life. In other words, the Bible is not written in mysterious, incomprehensible, mystical, language. Because we are made in the image of God, we should expect that God would communicate with us in the same ways that we communicate with each other.

So, for example, we see parents verbally authorizing certain behaviors and prohibiting others in various ways. So, how do parents do that? How do they indicate that some behaviors are mandatory, others are prohibited, and still others are optional? We can see that, to some extent, employers direct their employees, teachers instruct their students, and so forth, all in similar ways.

In other words, when we consider avenues of authority, we are not forcing some unnatural interpretations on the Bible. We are simply recognizing that the Holy Spirit used the very same communication tools that God gave us to use with each other. That does not mean that our task is easy. Rather, since this is the Word of God, we must apply all diligence (2 Timothy 2:15).

Let's consider various avenues of authority one by one. The first is direct statements.

Direct Statements

Many have said that the Bible authorizes through the use of commands, examples, and necessary inferences. That provides a good starting point. However, the idea of commands can be expanded to include all types of direct statements by which God expresses His authority.

Consider several kinds of direct statements, used both by parents and by God, to express His requirements, give His approval, indicate prohibitions, and/or give instructions.

【1】 **IMPERATIVE STATEMENTS** give specific commands. Parents may tell their teenager, "Get in there and clean up your room!" That's clear! Think of these command statements in the Bible:

Matthew 28:18-19

And Jesus came and spoke to them, saying, "All authority has been given to Me in heaven and on earth. Go therefore and make disciples of all the nations, baptizing them in the name of the Father and of the Son and of the Holy Spirit ...."

Acts 2:38

Then Peter said to them, "Repent, and let every one of you be baptized in the name of Jesus Christ for the remission of sins; and you shall receive the gift of the Holy Spirit."

2 Peter 3:17-18

You therefore, ... beware lest you also fall from your own steadfastness, being led away with the error of the wicked; but grow in the grace and knowledge of our Lord and Savior Jesus Christ. To Him be the glory both now and forever. Amen.

There are many specific commands in the Bible, and they are emphatically clear. However, we would be mistaken to think that commands are the only kinds of direct statements employed in scripture. Let us consider no less than seven other types.

{2} DECLARATIVE STATEMENTS authorize by stating facts. When parents say, for example, "It is your turn to wash the dishes," they mean, "Wash the dishes!" Likewise, note how the Bible reports facts that, in essence, authorize specific behaviors or responses.

John 4:24
God is Spirit, and those who worship Him must worship in spirit and truth.

Hebrews 11:6
But without faith it is impossible to please Him, for he who comes to God must believe that He is, and that He is a rewarder of those who diligently seek Him.

2 Corinthians 13:1
By the mouth of two or three witnesses every word shall be established.

{3} INTERROGATIVE STATEMENTS explain God's will by asking questions. When parents say, for example, "Who told you that you could wear that outfit?" they mean, "Change your clothes!" Likewise, the Bible also raises questions as a way of directing people in obedience.

Matthew 16:26

For what profit is it to a man if he gains the whole world, and loses his own soul? Or what will a man give in exchange for his soul?

Luke 6:46

But why do you call Me "Lord, Lord," and not do the things which I say?

Hebrews 2:3

... how shall we escape if we neglect so great a salvation, which at the first began to be spoken by the Lord, and was confirmed to us by those who heard Him?

[4] PRAYER STATEMENTS ask God regarding that which He would have happen in our lives. When parents pray for their children, for example, they may say, "I am praying that the Lord will help you be more patient and diligent." Think of the Bible's authorizations via prayer.

Philippians 1:9–11

And this I pray, that your love may abound still more and more in knowledge and all discernment, that you may approve the things that are excellent, that you may be sincere and without offense till the day of Christ, being filled with the fruits of righteousness which are by Jesus Christ, to the glory and praise of God.

1 Thessalonians 3:12

And may the Lord make you increase and abound in love to one another and to all, just as we do to you ....

[5] HORTATORY STATEMENTS ARE WORDS, often with "let us," that provide exhortation. When parents say, for example, "Let us go this way to be sure we get home on time," they are not offering a suggestion for consideration or for a vote! The Bible often exhorts Christians in this same way.

Galatians 6:9
And let us not grow weary while doing good, for in due season we shall reap if we do not lose heart.

1 Thessalonians 4:1
Finally then, brethren, we urge and exhort in the Lord Jesus that you should abound more and more, just as you received from us how you ought to walk and to please God; ....

Hebrews 6:1
Therefore, leaving the discussion of the elementary principles of Christ, let us go on to perfection, not laying again the foundation of repentance from dead works and of faith toward God ....

Hebrews 10:19-25
Therefore, brethren, ... let us draw near with a true heart in full assurance of faith .... Let us hold fast the confession of our hope without wavering, for He who promised is faithful. And let us consider one another in order to stir up love and good works ....

[6] CONDITIONAL STATEMENTS SAY, "If this happens, then this other will happen or not happen." "Unless this happens, then this other will happen or not happen." Parents may say: "If you are not ready (unless you are ready) by 7:30, then you cannot go." The Word of God authorizes and prohibits attitudes and behaviors the very same way.

John 3:5

Jesus answered, "Most assuredly, I say to you, unless one is born of water and the Spirit, he cannot enter the kingdom of God."

2 Timothy 2:11–13

This is a faithful saying: For if we died with Him, we shall also live with Him. If we endure, we shall also reign with Him. If we deny Him, He also will deny us. If we are faithless, He remains faithful; He cannot deny Himself.

Hebrews 3:6

... but Christ as a Son over His own house, whose house we are, if we hold fast the confidence and the rejoicing of the hope firm to the end.

Hebrews 10:38

... But if anyone draws back, My soul has no pleasure in him.

{7} WISH STATEMENTS express desires that indicate what a person intends to authorize or prohibit. When parents say, "May you learn your lesson this time!" it is obvious what they are saying. The Bible uses similar statements, including what they wish *not* to happen.

Romans 6:1–2 (NAS)

What shall we say then? Are we to continue in sin so that grace may increase? May it never be! How shall we who died to sin still live in it?

Galatians 6:14 (NAS)

But may it never be that I would boast, except in the cross of our Lord Jesus Christ, through which the world has been crucified to me, and I to the world.

[8] PARABLE / story statements describe events in a person's life to give instruction to those who are listening. Parents may prohibit hitting by saying, "There was once a child who hit his little sister and was punished." Jesus used parables so often that He never taught without them (Mark 4:34). As you read His stories, write down what He was authorizing or prohibiting.

Matthew 13:44–46

The kingdom of heaven is like a treasure hidden in the field, which a man found and hid again; and from joy over it he goes and sells all that he has and buys that field. Again, the kingdom of heaven is like a merchant seeking fine pearls, and upon finding one pearl of great value, he went and sold all that he had and bought it.

Matthew 25:24

Then he who had received the one talent came and said, "Lord, I knew you to be a hard man, reaping where you have not sown, and gathering where you have not scattered seed. And I was afraid, and went and hid your talent in the ground. Look, there you have what is yours."

Luke 15:17–19

But when [the prodigal, wasteful son] came to himself, he said, "How many of my father's hired servants have bread enough and to spare, and I perish with hunger! I will arise and go to my father, and will say to him, 'Father, I have sinned against heaven and before you, and I am no longer worthy to be called your son. Make me like one of your hired servants.'"

Conclusion

To return to fresh waters, we must establish biblical authority, using the avenues of communication that God has supplied. Perhaps the most obvious way the beginning point has to do with imperative commands and other direct statements. When the Word of God speaks by these means, we can be sure that the "water" is safe to drink and to share. As we study the New Testament, we must continue to look for, examine, and seek to apply and obey such statements. We must ask ourselves regarding each passage, "What direct statements are here that indicate what God requires, allows, or prohibits?"

Questions for Thought and Discussion

1. How can we explain the Restoration Plea in a kind, fair way to various religious people?
2. Why would we expect the Bible's communication methods to parallel our own?
3. Why does Bible study require and deserve diligent, intensive effort?
4. How do parents, employers, teachers, and the police illustrate avenues of authority?
5. Discuss biblical authority by imperative statements and give additional examples.
6. Discuss biblical authority by declarative statements and give additional examples.

7. Discuss biblical authority by interrogative statements and give additional examples.

8. Discuss biblical authority by prayer statements and give additional examples.

9. Discuss biblical authority by hortatory statements and give additional examples.

10. Discuss biblical authority by wish statements and give additional examples.

11. Discuss biblical authority by parable / story statements and give additional examples.

12. How might this material improve your own personal Bible study?

13. How will you record and remember the Bible's direct statements and what they authorize?

Chapter 9
Fresh Waters: Examples
1 Corinthians 10:1–14

In the Sermon on the Mount (Matthew 5–7), Jesus Christ emphasized His commitment to the exclusive authority of scripture. He wanted His hearers to know that He had come to fulfill—to bring to its fullest expression--the Word of God. He said He did not come to minimize, weaken, or abolish biblical authority. In fact, He aimed to restore a proper understanding of God's Word regarding murder, adultery, oaths, retaliation, and treatment of one's enemies (Matthew 5:17–48).

Out of love and reverence for Christ and His desire for restoration, Christians seek to preserve and continue this same commitment to biblical authority. Doing so does not mean that one worships the Bible itself, but that one worships the Savior who gave the Bible and whom the Bible reveals. Insisting on biblical authority does not necessarily make one a legalist, a rationalist, or a Pharisee, any more than it made Christ a legalist, a rationalist, or a Pharisee.

The Lord always told the objective truth, even when it was hard for His hearers to accept it. At times His language was blunt, stern, and strong, especially when He was addressing the false ideas and practices of the religious establishment. Many took offense at His words, and the authorities eventually determined to crucify Him for the things He said. Yet, all He did was to tell the truth. He did so, not to alienate or antagonize others, but to make God's message plain. He loved lost people so much that He tried to correct and even rebuke their errors.

It is the goal of this study to follow His example. We as Christians must not present ourselves as better, smarter, or more sincere than others. Rather, we humbly seek to know, obey, and share the objective truth of God's Word. We ask that those who read this book will see that our intent is to follow Jesus and to help others to do so, by returning where fresh waters flow.

Examples in Scripture

In scripture God often expressed His authority through examples. Yes, as we have noted, God used commands and other kinds of direct statements, but we must not stop there. It would be a grave error to say, "Unless the Bible commands or prohibits something directly, in exact, unmistakable terms, we need not be concerned about it." On the contrary, even a cursory view of the Bible shows how God used examples to approve or deny various beliefs and behaviors.

Examples in the Gospels

Jesus often used examples. He recalled Noah and the Flood to warn His disciples to be ready for sudden judgment (Luke 17:26–27, cf. Genesis 6–8). Likewise, He spoke of the days of Lot and the downpour of fire and brimstone on Sodom (Luke 17:28–30, cf. Genesis 19). When He said simply, "Remember Lot's wife" (Luke 17:31–32), He was telling His disciples to flee from Jerusalem when destruction was near and not turn back as she had done (cf. Genesis 19:26).

While preaching in the synagogue in His hometown of Nazareth, Jesus drew two examples from the Old Testament prophets, Elijah and Elisha (Luke 4:25–27). In both cases He noted that God's blessing came to Gentiles, first a widow from Zarephath in Sidon (cf. 1 Kings 17:9ff), and then Naaman, a Syrian leper (cf. 2 Kings 5:1–14). In the same way, Jesus had performed His signs, not for the people of His own city of Nazareth, but for those in other places.

Sometimes Jesus would tell a story so that He could *create* an example from it. He described the behavior of the so-called "Good Samaritan" to an expert in the Law. When the expert identified the Samaritan as the true neighbor because he showed mercy to a half-dead Jew in the ditch, Jesus said, "Go and do likewise" (Luke 10:25–37).

Jesus also used negative examples, as if to say, "Don't do what someone else did!" In the Sermon on the Mount He said, "Do not sound a trumpet as the hypocrites do" (Matthew 6:2). He went on to forbid praying as the hypocrites did and as the heathen did (Matthew 6:5–8). He then created a positive example, when He said, "Pray, then, in this manner ..." (Matthew 6:9–15). Next, He again rejected the hypocrites' example regarding fasting (Matthew 6:16–18).

In other words, Jesus found biblical *authority* in biblical *examples*. And He created examples for His disciples in His stories. Of course, Jesus Himself *is* the prime example for Christians. When Peter exhorted persecuted Christians to endure suffering, keep the faith, and honor the Lord, he wrote by inspiration in 1 Peter 2:21, "For to this you were called, because Christ also suffered for us, leaving us an example, that you should follow His steps."

Here Peter used the Greek term *hypogrammos*. It's a compound word, which combines *hypo* ("under") with *grammos* ("writing"). In the ancient world, a child would observe letters on a slate and then copy them below. That is, they would "write under" the model letter until they duplicated it perfectly. As followers of Jesus, we seek to watch Him closely, know Him more fully, and then reproduce His character, His words, and His purpose in our own lives.

Examples in Acts

The Book of Acts records the events that transpired in the one original church of Jesus Christ. It covers the time when the waters were fresh indeed. For that reason, any attempt to restore God's design for the church must study Acts carefully for examples related to God's authority.

Some events in Acts, such as the choosing of a qualified apostle by casting lots to replace Judas (Acts 1:15–26), occurred only once and were not regarded as practices to be repeated. Likewise, the Pentecost miracle of Acts 2 with the "tongues as of fire" was not a regular experience. Peter implied in Acts 11:15–17 that the Spirit's outpouring at Cornelius's house had only occurred just one other time, at Pentecost.

Then there are events in Acts that, though they are repeated, apparently were limited to the first-century period, while the apostles were still present and the scriptures were not yet completed. These would include, not only the preaching in foreign languages, but also miraculous healings, miraculous escapes from prison and danger, miraculous exorcisms (casting out of evil spirits), visions, vocal messages from the Holy Spirit, and resurrections from the dead.

We noted in chapter seven that 1 Corinthians 13:9–10 announced the coming end of tongues and prophecy, which were part of that initial phase of the church. In addition, to be consistent, one who affirms tongues-speaking today must also affirm *all* the miraculous elements in Acts, including miraculous resurrections.

However, there are other events in Acts that seem to be presented as models or examples for the church in all ages. These include:

- Preaching centered on Jesus Christ: His identity, ministry, death, burial, resurrection, ascension, and return. Two examples are found in Acts 2:22–36 and Acts 13:16–41.
- The necessity and urgency of repentance and immersion (biblical baptism) for the forgiveness of sins. Such occurred the same day or the same night of one's first sense of conviction. Eight major cases of conversion in Acts make this clear. There are the thousands at Pentecost (Acts 2), the Samaritans (Acts 8:4–13), the Ethiopian treasurer (Acts 8:26–40), Saul of Tarsus (Paul) (Acts 9:1–19, 22:1–16, 26:1–23), Cornelius and his family (Acts 10:1–48), Lydia and her household (Acts 16:13–15), the Philippian jailer and his family (Acts 16:22–34), and the Corinthians (Acts 18:1–8).
- The apostles' teaching (doctrine), fellowship, breaking of bread, and prayers (Acts 2:42).
- Courage in the face of persecution, imprisonment, and martyrdom (Acts 4–5, 6–7).
- Appointing servants (deacons) to care for widows and other saints in need (Acts 6).
- Sharing one another's lives, blessings, hardships, and material needs. (Acts 11:27–30)
- Preaching and teaching in public and from house to house (Acts 20:20).
- The spreading of the gospel into new frontiers and across all barriers.

- Singing praises to God, no matter the circumstances, even in prison (Acts 16:22–25).
- The forming of new congregations to which new converts were added (Acts 13–19).
- The appointment of elders in every church to oversee and shepherd the flock (Acts 14:23).
- The breaking of bread, the Lord's Supper, on the first day of the week (Acts 20:7–8).
- The supporting of the needs of other congregations in times of distress.

Examples in the New Testament Letters

Paul used the Old Testament Israelites as an example to warn the Corinthians that those once saved were not necessarily always saved (1 Corinthians 10:1–14). The Israelites, delivered from Egyptian bondage, perished in the desert and never made it to the Promised Land. They craved evil things, practiced idolatry, committed sexual immorality, tested the Lord, and grumbled. Paul said, in effect, "Do not follow their example, or else this will happen to you!" Here he taught by example that Christians can abandon the faith, return to a life of sin, and be lost.

The writer of Hebrews used Esau, the brother of Jacob, as an example for Christians. Esau sold his birthright to Jacob for a bowl of stew (Genesis 25:27–34). Of course, we are not in his exact situation. Yet, Hebrews 12:15–17 draws the principle, teaching us not to be a "fornicator or profane person like Esau, who for one morsel of food sold his birthright."

James by inspiration used the prophets as an example of suffering and patience. He noted Job's endurance and its outcome as evidence of the Lord's compassion (James 5:10–11).

Distinctions

Sometimes a biblical example is a specific *practice* itself, such as repentance and immersion in water for the forgiveness of sins. At other times, the example may be the *principle* which a particular practice expressed. For instance, we imitate Noah, not by building an ark, but by acting out of faith to obey God and save our families (Hebrews 11:7).

The *practices* of washing guests' dirty sandaled feet in the home, anointing their heads with oil, and kissing them, expressed the *principles* of hospitality, fellowship, and humility (Luke 10:44–46, John 13:1–17, 1 Timothy 5:10, Romans 16:16, 1 Corinthians 16:20, 2 Corinthians 13:12, 1 Thessalonians 5:26, 1 Peter 5:14). Forbidding women to remove their traditional head coverings (the *practice*) reflected the *principle* of submission to their husbands (the *principle*).

Finally, we must distinguish what is *essential* (say, eating the Lord's Supper on the first day of the week) from what is *incidental* (say, eating it in an "upper room" near midnight) (Acts 20:7–8). Sufficient water is essential for baptism by immersion, but the location of that water, whether in Jerusalem (Acts 2:41) or beside a road (Acts 8:36), is incidental. We can often recognize the incidental elements by noticing their variety, such as the various locations for baptism.

Questions for Thought and Discussion

1. How did Jesus emphasize biblical authority in His Sermon on the Mount?
2. Why would Jesus not base His teachings on His own opinions or those of the crowd?
3. How did Jesus strongly defend scripture without being "Pharisaical" or "legalistic?"

4. How does the Restoration Plea parallel Jesus's emphasis?

5. Some claim only direct commands, not examples, express God's authority. Your response?

6. How did Jesus Himself justify the use of examples in His teaching?

7. How does Peter's sermon in Acts 2:22–36 serve as an example for preaching today?

8. What does the crowd's response (conviction, immediate repentance, and baptism) indicate?

9. What are the other seven cases of conversion noted in this chapter from the Book of Acts?

10. As you read Acts, what other examples for Christians and the church today do you see?

11. How did Paul make it clear that Christians could perish and miss the "Promised Land?"

12. How do we follow Noah's example in principle without building an ark in practice?

13. How can we distinguish what is essential from what is incidental?

Chapter 10
Fresh Waters: Implications
Mark 2:1–12

I n our everyday conversations, we express ourselves not only *explicitly*, by the exact words we use, but also *implicitly*, by the unspoken messages we communicate along with those words. For example, when a father tells his child, "Give the dog a bath," he authorizes the child *by implication* to get the necessary tools, to use the water hose and soap, to proceed in an appropriate manner, and to clean up afterward. He forbids the child *by implication* to cover the dog in mud!

Parents use implication all the time, and children learn to "hear" what their parents never actually said "in so many words." That is, children infer or draw inferences from what they hear. What is an inference? An inference is the counterpart to or "flipside" of an implication. An inference is a logical deduction or conclusion, not explicitly stated, but required by what *is* explicitly stated. If the inference is necessary, based on what is implied, then that inference is binding or authoritative. In this case, the child infers that he or she is being "told" to get the necessary tools, carry out the task, and clean up when finished.

Implications in Scripture

The Bible clearly authorizes and prohibits by means of implication. This is not a contrived, artificial, man-made method
of interpretation unique to the Restoration Plea. God expects
people to think, to interpret, and to use common sense to
understand what He wants. In the Bible, God often conveys
His will indirectly. We must carefully and prayerfully infer
what He has implied.

For example, the command to baptize implies the need
for sufficient water for immersion. The command to sing
implies that there must be a hymn chosen and someone to
lead it.

Implications in Jesus's Teaching

Jesus certainly respected the *explicit* statements of Scripture.
Whatever God said, that was the absolute truth. However, in
addition to quoting a particular text, Jesus drew out the
implicit truths that were embedded within, or that lay underneath, that text. Jesus treated these implications as just as
true, binding, and absolute as if they were stated explicitly.

Not only did Jesus reason this way Himself; He expected
His hearers to reason in the same way and to accept the
implied conclusions that He presented. In other words, in
Jesus's approach, He showed that reason is not a bad thing! It
is not wrong to use common sense and rationality when
discussing biblical authority. Doing so does not by itself make
one a "rationalist" who worships human logic or puts logic
beside or above the Word of God. Reason is a God-given
tool. Jesus expected (and required) His hearers to use that
tool.

Read Matthew 15:1–20 and Mark 7:1–23. From the Old
Testament command, "Honor your father and mother"

(Exodus 20:12), Jesus inferred (from the implication) that grown children must provide financially for their aging parents. To refuse to do so is to disobey the *implicit* (yet still authoritative) teaching of Scripture. Jesus also said, "What goes into a man's mouth does not make him 'unclean.'" Mark (by inspiration) adds, "Thus Jesus (*implicitly*) declared all foods 'clean'" (Mark 7:19). So, Christians today understand that they may eat pork, shellfish, and other foods that were once prohibited under Mosaic Law. This is true, though no scripture *explicitly* says, "Christians may eat bacon."

Read Matthew 19:1–12. Since God explicitly said that in marriage male and female become one flesh (Genesis 2:24), Jesus drew the implicit truth that marriage was permanent and not to be ended. "Therefore, what God has joined together, let man not separate" (Matthew 19:6). From Jesus's words, "except for sexual immorality" (Matthew 19:9), Christians today draw the implication that divorce and remarriage *are* allowed if the cause of divorce *is* sexual immorality.

Read Mark 2:1–12. Jesus raised a paralytic from his mat and used this explicit fact to imply necessarily that He also had authority to forgive sins. The forgiveness of the man's sins was not visible or tangible, but it was implicitly proven by the visible miracle of healing. If Jesus could heal the man, He must have had divine authority. Because of that, He could forgive sins.

Read Mark 12:13–17. From the explicit fact that a denarius (a Roman coin) contained the portrait and inscription of Caesar, Jesus drew the implication that the Jews must pay taxes.

Read Mark 12:18–27. From God's exact words to Moses, "I am (at present) the God of Abraham, Isaac, and Jacob" (Exodus 3:6), Jesus reasoned that these men were still alive in Moses' day, though they had physically died. From the fact that they were still alive, Jesus taught that there was life after death and that the Sadducees were wrong. Of course, the text in Exodus did not state *explicitly* that these men were still alive. The Sadducees were wrong because they failed to see an authoritative implication that lay underneath the text. Jesus held them responsible.

Implications in the New Testament Letters

There are many instances of implications throughout the New Testament. Paul quoted the words of Joel 2:32: "Whoever calls on the name of the Lord will be saved." From that he inferred that there must be faith, there must be hearing, there must be preaching, and there must be the sending of preachers (Romans 10:13–15). The writer of Hebrews 8:13 noted the explicit promise of a "new covenant" (Jeremiah 31:31). From that text he inferred and insisted that God had implicitly made the first covenant old and obsolete. From the reference to Abraham's one "seed" (Genesis 12:7), Paul drew the implicit connection to Christ (Galatians 3:16).

Principles and Specifics of Implications

Necessity: We must infer what God has implied in order to answer various questions. Does the Bible authorize the preaching of the Word in each Sunday's church assembly? Are Christians to pray, sing, give, and observe the Lord's Supper each first day of the week? May women serve as elders? May infants be baptized? May Christians pray to Mary and the "saints?"

Cautions: We must be careful! No Christian's reasoning process is infallible. Each must humbly admit his own bias, resist the temptation to rationalize what he already believes, and ask God for wisdom (James 1:5). No implication is valid unless the text requires and warrants it. One who imposes ideas upon (or inserts them into) the text is guilty of presumption. Christians must study and discuss their differences regarding implications, so as to come to a mutual understanding.

Expedient Means: The teachings of God's Word imply, and we must infer, that we are authorized to employ whatever tools and methods are necessary, fitting, and appropriate to carry out those teachings. We noted this principle in our illustration above. As the father implicitly authorized his son to get the things necessary to bathe the dog, so the Scriptures often authorize.

The Lord commissioned us to preach and teach the Word so that people may hear. Expedient means may include a microphone, a pulpit, and electric lights to facilitate preaching. We may prepare radio and television broadcasts and use billboards. We may cooperate with each other, financially or otherwise, to saturate our area with the gospel. We may establish Bible classes for various age groups. They may conduct special services at nursing homes and jails. We may use additional deacons and ministers to teach and train their young people.

God has instructed the church to sing. Songbooks, song-leaders, four-part harmony, and pitch are not excluded because they do not add to or substitute for singing. Instead, they serve as expedients to singing because they are subordinate to the command and assist in its fulfillment. The command to sing authorizes Christians to write songs, to conduct training classes in singing, etc.

We are to commemorate the death of Christ via the Lord's Supper. Christians must find suitable means by which to do so. They may choose to use metal trays and multiple vessels. They may decide to distribute the bread in one particular way or another.

Of course, Christians must be careful not to turn optional

expedients into hard-and-fast requirements. Commands never change, but the expedient ways of obeying commands are open to judgment and subject to change. Expedients, by their very definition, are not specifically mandated by scripture. The Bible does not require the church to have a church building, a baptistery, or contribution trays. Other congregations, or Christians in another culture, may choose different means, but equally acceptable means, to do the will of God.

Exclusion: When a father tells his son, "Play in the front yard," he excludes other options. While God's Word does authorize expedient means to carry out His instructions, it also forbids substitutes. When God specifies what we are to believe or practice, He excludes alternatives and additions. The Bible does not have to say, "Do not do all these other things instead." When God authorizes "X," by implication He prohibits "non-X." Here are some examples.

- Noah was to use "gopher" wood and set measurements (Genesis 6:14), with no substitutes.
- Women are not to be elders, because the New Testament specifies men (1 Timothy 3).
- Sprinkling is not valid, because the Greek word *baptizo* means "to immerse" (Romans 6:3–4).
- Infant baptism is forbidden, because one must be convicted of sin first (Acts 2:37–41).
- The Lord's Supper is not observed on Tuesdays, because the early church met on the first day of the week to break bread (Acts 20:7; 1 Corinthians 11:17–34, 16:1–2).
- Denominational names are rejected, because of the name of Christ (1 Corinthians 1:10–13).
- Creeds and confessions, whether Catholic or Protestant, cannot be bound on men because the

Scriptures are complete and all-sufficient (2 Timothy 3:16–17).

- There is to be no super-church hierarchy, but rather elders in every church (Acts 14:23).
- Non-biblical names and titles such as "Reverend," "Monsignor," and "Father" are excluded.
- The Bible specifies vocal music (singing), thus excluding mechanical music.
- Overseers (elders) must be married men with children (1 Timothy 3:1–7). Others are excluded.

Silence: There are two important sides to understanding the Bible's silence, and we have hinted at them both by discussing expedients and exclusions. On the one hand, when God specifies what He wants, His silence as to our choice of expedient means is *permissive*. We are not adding to God's Word or misusing its silence, for example, when we build a pulpit for preaching, though the Bible is silent about building pulpits. On the other hand, when God specifies what He wants, His silence as to alternatives, additions, and substitutions is *prohibitive*. Therefore, we are not allowed to add items to the Lord's Supper, substitute sprinkling for baptism, or pray to Mary, though the Bible does not verbally and specifically prohibit these things.

Conclusion

The matter of establishing biblical authority by means of necessary implications and inferences is arguably the most challenging and controversial of all. Not everyone will agree easily and quickly as to what constitutes a *necessary* conclusion. In the following chapters, we will attempt to apply these principles to several key doctrinal areas.

Questions for Thought and Discussion

1. When a physician prescribes a medication, what does he implicitly authorize and prohibit?
2. How did Jesus use reason and expect others to use reason when interpreting scripture?
3. What did Jesus infer about marriage from Genesis 2:24?
4. What did Jesus infer about life after death from God's statement in Exodus 3:6?
5. "We must carefully aim to *draw from* the text and never to *inject into* the text." Discuss.
6. Why must we always be cautious and humble as we use our God-given reasoning?
7. How can we be "silent where the Bible is silent" and yet have baptisteries and hymnals?
8. Explain the principle of exclusion, and use Noah's "gopher" wood as an example.
9. In what sense is the Bible's silence permissive?
10. In what sense is the Bible's silence prohibitive?
11. Name some Christian beliefs and practices that are authorized by implication.
12. How can we address disagreements about what implications and inferences are "necessary"?
13. Baptism is authorized by all three: command, example, and implication. Give evidence.

Chapter 11
Fresh Waters: Covenant
Hebrews 8:1–13

J esus Christ said: "The Law and the Prophets were proclaimed until John. Since that time, the good news of the kingdom of God is being preached ..." (Luke 16:16). He drew a dividing line between the time the old covenant was in force and the time that John the Baptist began preparing people for the gospel and the kingdom.

Jesus taught that, unlike the Law of Moses, His new covenant would not restrict worship to any one specific place (John 4:19–26). He declared all foods to be "clean," even the "unclean" foods under Jewish Law (Mark 7:19; see Leviticus 11). He claimed to fulfill the old covenant through His coming, His ministry, His death, and His resurrection (Luke 24:25–27, 44–49).

He offered a new covenant, inaugurated and secured through the shedding of His blood (Luke 22:20). He sent His disciples, not to proclaim the Law of Moses, but to preach the gospel. The disciples announced that Christ had fulfilled the Law and the Prophets and that He had brought the gospel to take its place, for all people and for all time (Acts 13:13–52).

Old Testament Authority

As we discuss biblical authority, we must ask: "In what way, if any, does the Old Testament have authority in the church and in the Christian life today?" More specifically, one may ask, "Should the church observe the seventh day of the week as the Sabbath? Should the church have a separate priesthood of men, with special robes and titles? Should the church include incense, bells, and trumpets, or other musical instruments, in its worship? Does Old Testament circumcision authorize the church to 'baptize' infants by sprinkling?"

There are denominations that practice some of these things today, and they claim biblical (Old Testament) authority for them. If they are right, are others of us not wrong to reject these practices? If they are wrong, and the Old Testament does not authorize these things, then observing these practices is wrong. So, what role does the Old Testament play today? Why do we even need it? The emphasis of this chapter is this: the general *principles* of the Old Testament continue to teach the church, but the church is not to continue its specific religious *practices*.

When one U.S. President finishes his term and is replaced, this nation comes under a new administration. The basics presumably do not change, but the specific ways of implementing the basics do change. So it is with the Old Testament and the New Testament. The basics remain: the nature of God, the sinfulness of man, the need for grace, the need for sacrifice, the reverence and joy of worship, the importance of faith and obedience, the promise of judgment, etc.

However, the specific ways in which these elements are expressed have changed. The church is under the New Testament administration. The church is a New Testament fellowship of people that did not exist during the Old Testament era. Even so, the church can and must still learn from, and be guided by, the general principles and truths of the Old Testament.

The Early Christians' "Bible"

All Scripture is God-breathed (inspired) and profitable for teaching, reproof, correction, and instruction in righteousness (2 Timothy 3:16–17). The Old Testament was the only "Bible" that the first Christians had, and they used it and learned from it extensively. As we noted previously in this book, the Old Testament record provides examples both to encourage and to warn Christians today. Paul, in 1 Corinthians 10:1–14, used Israel's failure to teach the church not to imitate their example and thereby forfeit the Promised Land.

Just as God's nature does not change, neither does His moral standard. Idolatry, adultery, theft, etc., are just as wrong today as they were then. Those moral commandments still apply, and they express the unchanging command to love one's neighbor as oneself (Romans 13:8–10). In fact, Romans 15:4 indicates that everything written in the Old Testament was written for our learning, that we through the patience and comfort of the Scriptures might have hope.

So, the church must not ignore the Old Testament or minimize its importance. It is the vital foundation on which the New Testament rests. It promises and prepares for that which the New Testament provides and fulfills. The church, though it is a New Testament entity, believes, loves, and cherishes the Old Testament.

Principles, not Practices: the Book of Hebrews

Yet, while Christians are exhorted to imitate the faith of Old Testament characters, Christians are not commanded to do precisely what they did. Noah built a boat. Abraham traveled to a destination unknown to him. He offered his son as a sacrifice. Moses's parents hid their child. The Israelites kept the Passover, crossed the Red Sea, and circled the walls of Jericho.

Using specific Old Testament examples, the book of Hebrews calls Christians to:

- Pay more careful attention (2:1–4)
- Not harden their hearts (3:12–13)
- Believe and obey (3:18–19)
- Fear because they might miss the promised rest (4:1)
- Imitate those who through faith and patience inherited God's promises (6:12)
- Trust God's promises (6:13–20)
- Heed the words of Christ (10:26–31)
- Respect the blood that sanctifies (10:26–31)
- Live by faith (11)
- Accept God's discipline (12:3–11)
- Not refuse the One who speaks (12:18–29)

At the same time, the book of Hebrews never tells the church to observe the sacrifices, rituals, food laws, Sabbath days, or other specific requirements of the Old Testament. It says instead that, with a change of the priesthood, there also had to be a change of the law (7:12). When God promised a new covenant, He made the old covenant "obsolete." That which is obsolete and aging is ready to disappear (8:13). As an analogy, when a person says, "I need a new house," he implies that his old house has outlived its usefulness and must be replaced.

The tabernacle was a temporary copy of the true sanctuary in heaven (9:11). Since Christ entered the true sanctuary, the copy is no longer needed. The Law was only a shadow, not the reality (10:1). Now that the reality is here, no one should return to the shadow by practicing the Old Testament law. Old Testament sacrifices could not take away sin (10:1–4). Because Christ's one sacrifice did take away sin, there is no longer any need (or authority) for offering animals. These sacrifices pointed to Christ and ended with His death (10:11–14). Christ is the new, final, permanent High Priest (4:14–16, 5:1–8, 7:11–28). The church has no other High Priest.

A Specific People, a Limited Time

In other places, the New Testament indicates that the ritual practices of the Old Testament were designed for a specific people (Israel, not the whole world) and for a limited time (until its fulfillment in Christ). This is clear, for example, in Acts and in Galatians.

In Acts 15 some believers who were Pharisees wanted to require Gentiles to be circumcised and obey the Law of Moses (v. 5). If the specific teachings of the Old Testament had been intended to be universal and permanent, the apostles and elders would have agreed. However, they clearly refused this argument. Peter said instead, referring to the Old Testament law, "Now then, why do you try to test God by putting on the necks of the disciples a yoke that neither we nor our fathers have been able to bear?" (v. 10)

In the book of Galatians, Paul by inspiration addressed this controversy. He spoke of these Judaizers (those who would require Gentile Christians to observe Old Testament practices) as those who were "trying to pervert the gospel of Christ" (1:6–9). He said, "Through the law I died to the law so that I might live for God" (2:19). He wrote, "All who rely on observing the law are under a curse" (3:10), because the law demanded 100% perfect compliance and did not provide a Savior. He said that the law was given to a specific nation

(Israel, not the Gentiles) and that it served a temporary purpose (to show the Jews their need for Christ).

He wrote: "So the law was put in charge to lead us to Christ, that we might be justified by faith. Now that faith has come, we are no longer under the supervision of the law" (3:24–25). He said that both Jews and Gentiles were "children of Abraham," not because of their being circumcised or keeping the law of Moses, but because of their faith and baptism into Jesus Christ (3:26–29). He condemned the Judaizers for demanding that the Gentiles follow the law (5:12).

Death to the Law, Marriage to Christ

Paul made a similar point in Romans 7:1–4, saying that the law has no authority over one who has died, and that the Christian has "died" to the law and has become "married" to Christ. He contrasted the Old Testament (tablets of stone, death, and fading glory) with the New Testament (tablets of human hearts, the Spirit, and lasting glory) in 2 Corinthians 3:1–18. Christ "abolished in His flesh ... the law of commandments by the cross" (Ephesians 2:15–16). Christ removed the "handwriting of ordinances by nailing it to His cross" (Colossians 2:14). No one was to be allowed to condemn the Christians for what they ate or drank (dietary laws); religious festivals and the seventh-day Sabbath were not to be bound on them (Colossians 2:16). The New Testament sets apart the first day of the week, the day of Jesus's resurrection, as the Lord's Day (Luke 24:1, Acts 20:7, 1 Corinthians 16:1, Revelation 1:10). The church began on Pentecost, which always fell on Sunday (Acts 2:1).

Conclusion

When we say that there is no New Testament authority for the Saturday Sabbath, for a separate priesthood, or for incense and mechanical instruments in church worship, we are not rejecting the inspiration, truthfulness, or lasting value of the Old Testament. Rather, we are recognizing a change in matters of faith and practice that are part of a new administration. We preach and learn from the Old Testament, but it does not serve as our law.

Questions for Thought and Discussion

1. State in your own words the question that this lesson raises and addresses.
2. Why is this question so important? What kinds of things does it affect?
3. How does the Old Testament set the stage for, and prepare for the New Testament?
4. List unchanging Old Testament principles regarding the nature of God, man, sin, and grace.
5. What did Jesus say about the change of covenant from the Old to the New?
6. Explain the analogy used regarding the transition from one U.S. President to another.
7. When Hebrews 8 (Jeremiah 31) notes a "new" covenant, what does that imply?
8. When a man writes a new will or testament, does his earlier will remain in force?
9. Using Hebrews, distinguish Old Testament principles from specific requirements.
10. Why does the church desperately need to hear, study, and believe the Old Testament today?

11. What was the purpose of the Old Testament
    (Galatians 3:24–25)?
12. To whom was it given? For how long (Galatians
    3:24–25)?
13. Why do we not practice Old Testament worship,
    with sacrifices, incense, and instruments?

Chapter 12
Fresh Waters: Salvation
Titus 3:3–8

When John saw Jesus Christ coming toward him, he said, "Look, the Lamb of God, who takes away the sin of the world!" (John 1:29). Centuries before this time, God had graciously saved the Hebrews in Egypt who slaughtered lambs and put the blood on their doorposts. When the Lord saw the blood, He "passed over" the Jews and spared their firstborn (Exodus 12:12–13). The Jews were to observe the Passover annually, offering their lambs and looking forward to the ultimate "Lamb of God," the Messiah who would offer Himself on the cross as their scapegoat.

John identified Jesus as that Lamb, which all the Passover lambs through all the years since the Exodus foreshadowed and anticipated. Because of the blood of Christ, the perfect Lamb, God today passes over guilty sinners who deserve to die.

That is the heart of the plan of salvation. It is God's plan, not man's. It is rooted in God's mercy, not man's merit. It is the result of God's power, not man's perfection. It springs from God's grace, not man's goodness.

The blood of Christ purchased freedom from sin and its

consequences. That blood, and only that blood, is sufficient. One can be confident of his salvation and clear in his conscience because he knows that the blood covers him. All the emphasis, all the credit, and all the glory belong to Jesus Christ. His sacrifice for sin is the only ground on which anyone can stand before the holy God and not be consumed. Let there be no mistake: God does the saving. He alone provides the Lamb. He Himself bears the weight of sin and pays its penalty.

The analogy of Jesus as the Lamb of God can be taken a step further. Though the Hebrews in Egypt could not *achieve* their deliverance by their own strength, they were required to *receive* divine deliverance by faith. They were commanded to express that faith as God instructed them, or else perish with the Egyptians. To kill a lamb and put its blood over one's door was not a meritorious act that earned salvation, but an obedient extension of faith in the grace of God, who released the faithful Hebrews from death.

The Scripture says,

> For it is by grace you have been saved, through faith—and this not from yourselves, it is the gift of God—not by works, so that no one can boast. For we are God's workmanship, created in Christ Jesus to do good works, which God prepared in advance for us to do (Ephesians 2:8–10).

In other words, the grace of God (found in the cross of Christ) is the **ground or basis** of salvation. Faith is the **means or avenue** through which one receives salvation. Good works are the **fruit or consequences** that result from salvation. One is not saved on the basis of his worthy works. Rather, one works because he is saved by the grace of God through his faith.

Roots, Trunk and Branches, and Fruit

Picture a tree, which has roots, a trunk and branches, and fruit. The roots represent the ground of salvation, the cross of Christ. The trunk and branches represent the faith that is grounded in the cross and receives its life from the cross. The fruit represents the godly, Christ-like life that results from the connection of the trunk and branches to the roots.

Jesus used this same type of analogy in John 15:1–8. There He said that He was the vine, that His followers were the branches, and that fruit was the indisputable evidence that a branch was connected to the vine. The source of the fruit is the vine itself. Because the branch abides in the vine, it becomes the necessary means through which the fruit is produced.

The Man Born Blind

Jesus's healing of the man born blind, recorded in John 9:1–12, clearly illustrates and keeps in perspective these three concepts: ground, means, and fruit. Read the text and notice them. First, what was the ground of the healing? The man received his sight by the grace of God, not by his own worth or merit. Second, what was the means? He received his sight by faith, which he expressed (as commanded) by washing in the pool of Siloam. Third, what was the fruit? He came back seeing, and he told others what the Lord had done for him.

No one could effectively argue that the man was healed because of his good works. No, the good works followed his healing. Neither could anyone say that he earned or accomplished his healing by washing himself in the pool of Siloam. That washing was simply an expression of faith in Jesus's promise. ***It was by means of faith, put into action in his*** *washing in the pool, that the man born blind received the gracious gift of healing. If the man had refused to wash, he would have shown that he did not have faith in Jesus's offer, and he would have remained blind. In the same way, a Hebrew who would not put lamb's blood over his door would thereby show his lack of faith in God's promise and warning, and his firstborn would have perished.*

A Prisoner Set Free

Imagine that a wealthy benefactor wants to give a check for $10 million to a debt-ridden prisoner in jail. That is grace, parallel to God's desire to give each person eternal life at the cost of His Son's life. However, the prisoner must trust the benefactor and show his faith by endorsing the check and depositing it in the bank. That is faith, parallel to man's response to the gospel.

After his release, the former prisoner spends his life in gratitude, committing himself to honor his benefactor and to become exactly like him in his attitude, words, and deeds. That is fruit, parallel to one's good works that result from his being saved by faith. The gift is of grace. One does not earn it by endorsing and depositing the check. On the other hand, unless and until he does so, he remains lost in his debt. The gift of grace is not his.

Because of, Through, and So That

One sees these concepts in Ephesians 2:8–10 and elsewhere. Notice Titus 3:3–8:

- **Ground:** "... he saved us, not because of righteous things we had done, but **because of** his mercy."

- **Means:** "He saved us ***through*** the washing of rebirth and renewal by the Holy Spirit ..." This is a reference to baptism, the new birth of water and the Spirit. See John 3:3–5.
- **Fruit:** "... stress these things, ***so that*** those who have trusted in God may be careful to devote themselves to doing what is good."

One Extreme: Man's Involvement Over-Emphasized

How does all of this relate to the Restoration Plea? First, consider two extremes that have developed regarding salvation. Then note the New Testament concepts that the church today seeks to restore.

As the Catholic Church evolved, so did a system of salvation that was based on human works of merit. If one observed the "seven sacraments," said all the prayers, and performed sufficient acts of righteousness, one was promised eternal life as a result. One could carry out acts of penance for specific sins. If a person died who was "not righteous enough" for heaven but was "too righteous" for hell, the person entered Purgatory. In Purgatory he or she would suffer a sufficient length of time to pay the remaining debt for his or her sins and would then be promoted to heaven. During the Middle Ages, the Catholic Church promised its members that, if they would contribute more money, they would shorten the length of time that their ancestors (currently in Purgatory) would have to suffer in the flames. People bought "indulgences," first to show repentance for their sins, and then as if they could "buy" a license to sin.

In other words, this system confused root and fruit. It made good works to be the basis, not the consequence, of eternal life. It led people to believe that if they were good enough, they could earn eternal life. If they sinned, they could make up for their sin by acts of personal righteousness. They acknowledged the cross and the suffering of Christ, but they left the impression that one ultimately saved himself by his own deeds.

These acts and sacraments were considered to have merit, even if one did not observe them as acts of personal faith. For example, the sacrament of baptism was administered to infants who had no faith, because the act itself was thought to be efficacious.

The Other Extreme: Man's Involvement Eliminated

Against this background, and as a reaction against it, some of the 16th-century Protestant reformers went to the opposite extreme. Repulsed by the Catholic idea of works salvation based on human ability, they practically removed the human element from salvation altogether!

John Calvin led the way, declaring that man was totally depraved and unable to have faith apart from a direct act of God. He proclaimed that God had unconditionally chosen and pre-determined each person who would be saved. He taught that God's grace would act irresistibly on that person's heart and produce faith. He also said that God would control the person's continuing faith and perseverance in the Christian life so that he could never fall away and be lost.

Whereas the Catholic system seemed to put the fruit of the tree where the root should be, the Calvinist system in effect removed the trunk from the tree. It emphasized divine sovereignty to such an extent that it eliminated one's personal choice to put one's faith in Christ. It redefined faith as that which God irresistibly planted in the hearts of those He selected and predetermined to save. Calvinism claimed that Christ did not die so that the whole world could be saved, but that He only died for the pre-selected few, to whom God would grant faith and perseverance aprior to their own will.

As a result of Calvinism, many people believe still today that [1] one does not have to be baptized or "do anything" to receive salvation, [2] one is "born again" when he experiences God's inner work in his heart, and [3] once one is saved, he can never be lost. The devastating influence of John Calvin and those who have promoted his beliefs cannot be measured.

The New Testament acknowledges the grace of God as the basis of salvation and faith as the means of receiving salvation. It holds *man* responsible, not God, for man's faith or lack of faith (John 8:24). It says that one must express his faith in Christ by confessing Him before men (1 Timothy 6:12), repenting of his sins (Luke 24:47), and being immersed (baptized) into His death and resurrection (Acts 2:38, Romans 6:3–4). It presents good works, not as the basis of salvation, but as its inevitable and essential fruit. It states that one who abandons his faith falls away from God and faces His eternal judgment (Hebrews 10:26–31).

Questions for Thought and Discussion

1. How did John first identify Jesus? Why is that significant?
2. Though salvation cannot be earned by human effort, must it still be received?
3. How did the Hebrews express their faith? What if they had not done so?
4. Describe the three parts of a tree, and relate them to salvation.
5. According to Jesus, are good works ("fruit") the *basis* or the *result* of one's salvation?

6. On what basis did the blind man in John 9 receive his sight? By whose power?

7. How was he to express his faith? If he had not obeyed, would he have received his sight?

8. Paraphrase the message of Titus 3:3-8 in your own words.

9. Discuss the first extreme error: making good works the *root* rather than the *fruit*.

10. If one's own works could earn salvation, did Christ really have to die?

11. Discuss the second extreme error: effectively removing man's choice and responsibility.

12. Are all people free, responsible, and required to repent and be baptized to be saved?

13. What will happen to one who abandons his or her faith in Christ after once being saved?

Chapter 13
Fresh Waters: Conversion
1 Thessalonians 1:6–10

In our fervent desire to return to the fresh waters God provides, we cannot emphasize enough the importance of personal conversion. Conversion is one's all-or-nothing, life-or-death, no-matter-what decision to follow Jesus Christ as His disciples. We dare not "check off" outward elements as some kind of substitute for the inward faith, hope, and love that they express. We must learn from ancient Israel and from the Pharisees just how real and tempting that trap may be.

When Jesus invited four fishermen to follow Him (Mark 1:16–20), they had to make a decision, a single decision that would determine everything about their lives. So it is with us today. When Paul recalled the Thessalonians' response to the gospel, he wrote,

> ... you turned to God from idols to serve the living and true God, and to wait for His Son from heaven, whom He raised from the dead, even Jesus who delivers us from the wrath to come (1 Thessalonians 1:9–10).

Cases of Conversion in Acts

Eight occasions in the Book of Acts describe how sinners, convicted of their sin by the preaching of the gospel, responded and converted to Christ. As a result, they tasted the fresh, pure waters of salvation by grace through faith, when they expressed their faith as God directed.

1. The crowd on the Day of Pentecost—Acts 2:14–41

On Pentecost Sunday, some fifty days after the Passover Sabbath when Jesus's body was in the tomb, Peter stood with the other apostles and preached the gospel to thousands in Jerusalem. After explaining the outpouring of the Holy Spirit, he declared that Jesus had been attested by God through His undeniable miracles. The people had crucified Jesus, but God had raised Him from the dead as David had predicted about a thousand years earlier. Jesus had ascended, and God had exalted Him to His right hand, making Him both Lord and Christ (Acts 2:22–36).

Many in the crowd were convicted and cut to the heart. They were crushed by the realization that they had crucified the very One that God had sent to save them. Without that conviction, there could be no conversion. They were ready to turn, but how could they be free of their past? Was there any hope or remedy? They cried out in despair, "What shall we do?"

In unmistakable terms, Peter said, "Repent, and let every one of you be baptized in the name of Jesus Christ for the remission of sins; and you shall receive the gift of the Holy Spirit" (Acts 2:38). What amazing news! These complicit murderers could receive forgiveness, freedom, and the gift of the Holy Spirit, all at no cost. They could not buy or earn this salvation, but they were required to repent and be immersed (baptized) in order to claim it as their own.

Peter continued to offer them this invitation, even exhorting them urgently to "be saved;" they were convicted but not yet converted (Acts 2:40). Then, "those who gladly received his word were baptized; and that day about three thousand souls were added to them" (Acts 2:41). That first congregation of disciples then began devoting themselves to the things of God.

According to the text, when were they forgiven of their sins? When did they receive the gift of the Holy Spirit? When were they added together as a unit? These things occurred only after, and not before, their repentance and baptism.

This phrase, "for the remission of sins," cannot mean, "because your sins are already forgiven." Jesus had spoken these same words at the Last Supper. His blood would be shed "for the remission of sins" (Matthew 26:28). He would die, not because sins were already forgiven, but in order that they could be forgiven. Therefore, "for the remission of sins" in Acts 2:38 explains the reason that lost sinners must repent and be baptized.

In previous chapters, we have noted that biblical authority is expressed through direct statements (including commands), approved examples, and necessary implications which we infer. Here in Acts 2, we see all three avenues of authority. Repentance and baptism were commanded, and they were exemplified. The necessary implication is that repentance and baptism were required for salvation, which is implied in the phrase, "the remission (or forgiveness) of sins."

Only those who are capable of repentance were eligible for baptism; therefore, infants were not to be baptized. In addition, we may infer that baptism was urgent since these thousands were baptized the same day, without delay. Also, since the Greek word *baptizo* meant to immerse, dip, or plunge,[1] we infer that these thousands were baptized by immersion, not by having water sprinkled or poured on them. By the way, archaeologists have uncovered at least fifty immersion pools (Hebrew, *mikvot)* in the area near the temple mount, where these baptisms likely occurred.[2]

2. The people of Samaria—Acts 8:5–13

After Stephen was arrested, put on trial, and martyred by stoning (Acts 6–7), there arose a great persecution against the church in Jerusalem. Many of the disciples were scattered (Acts 8:1–4). Philip went to the city of Samaria and proclaimed Christ to the people. Though they had previously followed a magician named Simon, they saw a greater power at work through Philip.

The scriptures say simply,

> But when they believed Philip as he preached the things concerning the kingdom of God and the name of Jesus Christ, both men and women were baptized. Then Simon himself also believed; and when he was baptized, he continued with Philip ... (Acts 8:12–13).

These were believing men and women, not infants incapable of faith.

3. The Ethiopian—Acts 8:26–40

This same Philip was then directed to go to a place where

---

1. William Arndt et al., *A Greek-English Lexicon of the New Testament and Other Early Christian Literature* (Chicago: University of Chicago Press, 2000), 164–165.

2. https://www.timesofisrael.com/immerse-yourself-in-the-holy-lands-history-by-visiting-these-ancient-ritual-baths/

he met an Ethiopian official, a eunuch who served as the trea-surer for his nation's queen. Though he was a Gentile, he had been to Jerusalem to worship and was now returning home. Reading aloud Isaiah's 700-year-old prediction of the One who would be slain as a lamb (Isaiah 53), the Ethiopian asked Philip to explain. Philip then began with that text and preached (Greek, "evangelized") Jesus to him.

As always, the emphasis was on Jesus Christ. The plan of salvation was first of all God's plan to send Jesus to save the world. At the same time, the eunuch understood from Philip's explanation that he was to respond in faith and obedience and without delay. Philip must have explained to him the purpose, necessity, and urgency of his response because as they went down the road, they came to some water. And the eunuch said, "See, here is water. What hinders me from being baptized?" (Acts 8:36) Some manuscripts of Acts record the Ethiopian's confession of his faith in Jesus Christ as the Son of God. Confession was certainly involved in New Testament conversions. See Acts 2:21, 22:16; Romans 10:9–10; and 1 Timothy 6:12–13. See also Jesus's teaching in Matthew 10:32–33. The Ethiopian stopped the chariot. He and Philip went down into the water, and he was immersed (Acts 8:38). Then he went on his way rejoicing (Acts 8:39).

The element in which baptism takes place is water. One is born again, not via some purely inward experience, but of water and the Spirit (John 3:5). The mode of baptism is immersion, not sprinkling or pouring. The word "baptism" is a transliteration of a Greek word meaning to immerse, dip, or plunge. The Greeks even today use this word to refer to ships that sink at sea.

4. Saul (Paul)—Acts 9:1–19, 22:1–16, 26:9–18

Saul of Tarsus, a violent enemy of Jesus's disciples, was stunned to see a light from heaven and hear the voice of Jesus Christ. However, though he had seen Jesus, though he believed, though he was blinded, and though he fasted for three days, Ananias still urged him, "And now what are you waiting for? Get up, be baptized and wash away your sins, calling on His name" (22:16). His sins were yet to be forgiven, at the point of his baptism and confession.

5. Cornelius, with his relatives and close friends—Acts 10:34–48

In order to convince Peter that Gentiles were eligible to be baptized and saved, God provided visions and even poured out the Holy Spirit. Cornelius the Roman centurion, with his relatives and friends, heard the gospel and believed (10:34–43). The Holy Spirit's sudden arrival (10:44–46) did not remove the necessity of baptism but rather revealed its urgency. Peter did not say they were saved without being baptized. Instead, he commanded that they be baptized at once (10:47–48).

6. Lydia and her household—Acts 16:13–15

At a prayer gathering beside a river in Philippi, a Jewish woman named Lydia listened to Paul's message. The Lord opened her eager, willing heart. She and her household with her were baptized. There is no reason to assume or imagine that unbelieving infants were included.

7. The Jailer in Philippi and his household—Acts 16:25–34

After casting out a spirit of divination, Paul and Silas were arrested and imprisoned. An earthquake broke their chains. The jailer woke up and asked, "What must I do to be saved" (Acts 16:30)? They told him to "believe" and that he and his household would thus be saved. But *how* were they to believe?First, they heard the word of God. Then the jailer washed their stripes; that is repentance. Then those capable of faith were baptized at once, even after midnight. As a result, he and his household rejoiced that they had "believed" in God (16:31–34).

8. The Corinthians—Acts 18:1–17

Paul traveled from Athens to Corinth, proclaiming the good news about Jesus. Scripture reports that "Crispus, the ruler of the synagogue, believed on the Lord with all his household. And many of the Corinthians, hearing, believed and were baptized" (Acts 18:8).

Confirmation of Conversion in the New Testament Letters

Romans 6:1–14 describes baptism is an immersion into union with the death, burial, and resurrection of Christ. At this point, one "dies" to sin and "rises" to new life in Christ. Before baptism one is dead *in* sin; after baptism, he is dead *to* sin.

1 Corinthians 10:1–2 presents God's bringing Israel from slavery to salvation through the Red Sea as a "baptism." 1 Corinthians 12:13 notes the Spirit's involvement in baptism, so

that each believer comes into the body of Christ at that point.

Colossians 2:11–12, 3:1–4 notes baptism as a "circumcision" in the sense that God removes his sin. "Buried with Him in baptism" and "raised with Him through faith" indicate that baptism is inseparably joined to faith as its necessary outward expression.

Galatians 3:26–27 teaches that one becomes a child of God by faith because that person clothes himself with Christ in baptism.

1 Peter 3:18–22 recalls God's having saved Noah and his family "through water." God still saves people today "through water." The water that saved Noah typifies or represents the water of baptism. In that sense, "baptism now saves you." Of course, it is God who saves, always by grace, always through faith, and always by bringing one through the water of baptism.

Questions for Thought and Discussion

1. Define conversion in your own words, emphasizing its radical significance.
2. Use the four fishermen and the Thessalonians to explain what real conversion involves.
3. Discuss the danger of substituting an external checklist for wholehearted conversion.
4. Discuss the opposite danger of rejecting the biblical external elements of conversion.
5. Why do some sincere religious people insist that baptism is not necessary for salvation?
6. In Acts 2, when the people were convicted of sin, what did Peter tell them to do?

7. When did they receive the forgiveness of sins and the gift of the Holy Spirit?

8. What did the Ethiopian want to do immediately after hearing the good news about Jesus?

9. After Saul's miraculous encounter with Jesus, what did Ananias urge him to do and why?

10. What did the Holy Spirit's arrival at Cornelius's house cause Peter to command at once?

11. How did the jailer "believe" in Jesus after midnight? Why was his response so urgent?

12. How did Peter use Noah's flood as a basis for saying, "Baptism now saves you?"

13. Is it harsh or judgmental to say that sincere people must still be baptized to be saved?

Chapter 14
Fresh Waters: the Memorial
1 Corinthians 11:17–34

The night before He died, at the Passover meal with His disciples,

> ... Jesus took bread, blessed and broke it, and gave it to the disciples and said, "Take, eat; this is My body." Then He took the cup, and gave thanks, and gave it to them, saying, "Drink from it, all of you. For this is My blood of the new covenant, which is shed for many for the remission of sins" (Matthew 26:26–28).

In God's timing, the spotless Lamb of God would be sacrificed so that God would "pass over" the sins of those who are covered by the blood. One may read about the Passover in Exodus 12.

The Lord's Supper

This simple memorial commemorates and proclaims the death of Christ. It draws the Christian back to the cross. It calls for personal self-examination, self-judgment, and repentance. It rekindles one's fire of devotion and love for the Savior. It renews one's appreciation for His gracious sacrifice and the freedom of forgiveness that results (1 Corinthians 11:17–34).

The serious significance of this memorial cannot be overstated. One who merely partakes as a matter of routine, not taking inventory of his own sin and need for grace, partakes in an unworthy manner and is therefore "guilty of the body and the blood of the Lord" (1 Corinthians 11:27). "Discerning the body" may refer to considering the body of Christ as He died. It may also refer to thinking of the church (the body of Christ) and one's own role in it.

In addition, the Christian's participation at the Lord's table necessarily implies a rejection and repudiation of all competing allegiances. The bread and the cup are a "communion," that is, a sharing, fellowship, or partnership, with the body and the blood of Christ. Therefore, one must not compromise or diminish that exclusive relationship in any way. In fact, doing so would provoke the Lord to jealousy. Read carefully 1 Corinthians 10:14–22 regarding this matter.

Unleavened Bread and the Fruit of the Vine

During the context of the Passover meal, Jesus chose just two elements for the future memorial, unleavened bread and the fruit of the vine. In Corinth, the church had included a meal, which left some hungry and others drunk! In response, Paul wrote, "What? Do you not have houses in which to eat and drink?" (1 Corinthians 11:20–22) He went on to clarify the fact that the Lord's Supper was to involve just the bread and the cup (1 Corinthians 11:23–26).

Virtually all religious groups that claim to follow Christ have recognized the exclusive nature of biblical silence in this matter. Since God specified just these two elements, nothing is to be added, removed, or substituted. In this case, they know that biblical silence is prohibitive. To return to fresh waters, we must also respect God's exclusive authorization in other matters, such as baptism only by immersion and only for penitent believers who seek to be saved.

The fact that the bread is to be unleavened is significant. Of course, the Jews were commanded to use unleavened bread when leaving Egypt in their haste (Exodus 12:15), and Jesus used the same at the Last Supper. In addition, the New Testament uses the absence of leaven to represent the rejection of sin. After instructing the church to purge the "leaven" of sin, Paul wrote that Christians are to be "unleavened." Then he added, "For indeed Christ, our Passover, was sacrificed for us. Therefore let us keep the feast, not with old leaven, nor with the leaven of malice and wickedness, but with the unleavened bread of sincerity and truth" (1 Corinthians 5:6–8).

The phrase "the fruit of the vine" (Matthew 26:29, Mark 14:25, Luke 22:18) may have been just grape juice. It must not be understood to justify any level of intoxication. The light "wine" of Jesus's day was typically mixed with large amounts of water in order to avoid such effects. The process of distillation, which would produce the kind of concentrated alcohol common today, was not known until the Arabs invented it in the Middle Ages, according to R. Laird Harris.[1]

Jesus said, "This is My body," and, "This is My blood." Not seeing these as metaphors, the Roman Catholic Church made transubstantiation (meaning a change of substance) an official doctrine at the Fourth Lateran Council in AD 1215. Supposedly, when blessed, the bread and the cup were miraculously

---

1. R. Laird Harris, "864 יָן," in *Theological Wordbook of the Old Testament*, ed. R. Laird Harris, Gleason L. Archer Jr., and Bruce K. Waltke (Chicago: Moody Press, 1999), 37.

changed into the literal, physical body and blood of Christ. Yet it was claimed that the appearance, texture, and taste of these elements would remain unchanged.

Some have insisted that the words, "the cup" and "the one bread" (1 Corinthians 10:16-17), require one vessel and one loaf for the entire church. Not the entire church worldwide, of course, but each congregation would presumably have its own single cup and single loaf. Even that would be impossible once a congregation reached a very large size, as the Jerusalem church numbered in the thousands (Acts 4:4). So, it must be possible to use multiple vessels for the one worldwide "cup of the Lord" and multiple loaves of bread for the bread as well.

On the First Day of the Week: the New Testament Evidence

During Paul's third missionary journey, recorded in Acts 18:23–21:17, he and the mission team arrived in Troas in Macedonia. After seven days there, and not before, "... on the first day of the week, when the disciples came together to break bread, Paul, ready to depart the next day, spoke to them and continued his message until midnight" (Acts 20:7).

Though "break bread" in other contexts may refer simply to a shared meal (Mark 6:41, 8:6), that cannot be the case here. In this situation, this breaking of bread occurred only on the one day, the first day of the week. It was stated to be the purpose of the disciples coming together, and it was accompanied by Paul's preaching. In other words, it was a worship setting.

We infer from this scripture that the first day of the week was the day of worship on which the church assembled. We infer further that the disciples observed the Lord's Supper on that day in memory of Jesus Christ, as He had directed when He first instituted it.

Other scriptures confirm these inferences. It is evident from 1 Corinthians 11 that, though the Lord's Supper had been abused and corrupted, its observance was intended to be part of the central focus of the church's assembly. The Christians were to honor, not only the form of the Lord's Supper, with the bread and the cup, but also its function. "For as often as you eat this bread and drink this cup, you proclaim the Lord's death till He comes" (1 Corinthians 11:26).

"As often as" cannot mean "as often as you choose, on whatever day you choose." That would contradict the approved example found in Acts 20:7, where the disciples waited seven days to break bread specifically on the first day of the week. In addition, "as often as" corresponds to the first-day every-week meeting at which the collection was taken (1 Corinthians 16:1–2).

Why the first day of the week? First of all, that was the day on which Christ arose from the dead. On that same evening, Jesus met with all His disciples except Thomas (John 20:19–25). Then it was on the first day of the *following* week that Jesus met with them again, this time with Thomas present (John 20:26–29). In addition, it was on Pentecost, which was always on the first day of the week, that the events of Acts 2 took place, including the beginning of the church.

Why not the Sabbath? The New Testament is very clear as to why Christians are not to be compelled to observe the seventh day of the week as the Israelites were to do during the Old Testament era. Paul told the church in Colossae that Christ had nailed the Old Testament decrees to His cross (Colossians 2:14). Then he wrote specifically regarding those ordinances, "So let no one judge you in food or in drink, or regarding a festival or a new moon or sabbaths, which are a shadow of things to come, but the substance is of Christ" (Colossians 2:16–17).

Though Paul and others went into various Jewish synagogues on Sabbath days (Acts 9:20; 13:14ff; 17:1-4, 10, 17), they did so for the purpose of evangelism. They took these opportunities to proclaim the message of the Messiah (Christ) to the Jews and the God-fearing Gentiles present.

The idea that the Roman Catholic Church somehow replaced the seventh-day Sabbath with the first day of the week as the church's day of worship is false. There is just no evidence for this. In addition, note the words "the Lord's Day" in Revelation 1:10. The Greek term used here is the very same term used in the Greek language today for Sunday, the first day of the week.

On the First Day of the Week: the Historical Evidence

Early, uninspired Christian writings confirm the point. The *Didache,* written c. AD 90–110, noted: "But on the Lord's day, after that ye have assembled together, break bread and give thanks, having in addition confessed your sins, that your sacrifice may be pure." [2] Ignatius (d. AD 110) wrote: "... no longer observing the Sabbath but living according to the Lord's Day, in which also our life arose through him and his death (which some deny) ..."[3]

The *Epistle of Barnabas* (c. AD 80–120)

> ... I will make the beginning of the eighth day which is the beginning of another world. Wherefore also we keep the eighth day for rejoicing, in the which also Jesus rose from the dead, and having been manifested ascended into the heavens.[4]

---

2. Charles Hoole, trans., *The Didache: The Teaching of the Lord to the Gentiles through the Twelve Apostles.* (WORDsearch, 1900).

3. *The Epistle of Ignatius to the Magnesians,* 9.

4. *The Epistle of Barnabas,* 15:8–9.

Justin Martyr (AD 150) wrote:

> ... And on the day called Sunday there is a gathering together in the same place of all who live in a city or a rural district. ... We all make our assembly in common on the day of the Sun, since it is the first day, on which God changed the darkness and matter and made the world, and Jesus Christ our Savior arose from the dead on the same day.
>
> There is then brought to the presider of the brethren bread and a cup of wine mixed with water; and he taking them, gives praise and glory to the Father of the universe, through the name of the Son and of the Holy Ghost, and offers thanks at considerable length for our being counted worthy to receive these things at His hands. And when he has concluded the prayers and thanksgivings, all the people present express their assent by saying Amen. And when the presider has given thanks, and all the people have expressed their assent, those who are called by us deacons give to each of those present to partake of the bread and wine mixed with water over which the thanksgiving was pronounced, and to those who are absent they carry away a portion. For they crucified him on (Friday) the day before Saturn's day, and on the day after (which is the day of the Sun) he appeared to his apostles.[5]

Questions for Thought and Discussion

1. Why is it significant that Jesus instituted the Lord's Supper at the time of the Passover?
2. Why is it crucial that Christians observe the Lord's Supper with the proper attitude?

---

5. *Apology* I, 67:1–3, 7.

3. How can Christians avoid making the Lord's Supper a simple matter of rote routine?

4. How does 1 Corinthians 10:14–22 tie the Lord's Supper to exclusive allegiance to Christ?

5. Why would it be wrong to add to, take away from, or substitute for the bread and the cup?

6. What point did Paul use the "unleavened" bread to make?

7. What is transubstantiation? How does that teaching misunderstand metaphors?

8. Discuss the idea that the church worldwide drinks from one cup, but in multiple vessels.

9. Why did the New Testament church worship on the first day rather than the Sabbath?

10. What does the approved example in Acts 20:7 indicate about the Lord's Supper?

11. Why does the phrase "as often as" point to observing the Lord's Supper every week?

12. How would you show that the Catholic Church did not choose the first day of the week as the day for Christian worship?

13. Discuss the writings of the *Didache,* the *Epistle of Barnabas,* and Justin Martyr that are related to early Christian worship.

Chapter 15
Fresh Waters: Adoration
Ephesians 5:15–21

After the Last Supper, Jesus and His disciples sang a hymn (Matthew 26:30). With remarkable simplicity, these men lifted up their voices in worship and praise to God. When Paul and Silas were later imprisoned in Philippi, they were beaten severely. Yet at midnight they were "praying and singing hymns to God ..." (Acts 16:25). Here were two servants of Christ, in pain yet full of faith, adoring God in pure, unaccompanied, vocal praise.

To return to where fresh waters flow is to return to the faith, the fervor, the passion, and the simplicity of first-century worship in song. The church that excludes an organ or a band has not done so based on a man-made tradition. Rather, that church is going back to earlier days, to the New Testament pattern that existed before man's traditions added such instruments.

Biblical Support for Vocal Music

Jesus made it clear that the old temple system would give way to worship, not in a specific, required place, but rather "in spirit and truth" (John 4:19–24). The book of Hebrews emphasizes the changes from the Old to the New (Hebrews 8:13–10:18). While Christians learn from the Old Testament's unchanging principles, they do not follow its specific means of worship.

Incense, dancing, animal sacrifice, a separate priesthood, the Sabbath, three annual holy days, and instrumental music in the temple worship were all part of that past administration. Read 2 Chronicles 29:20–36 and note that only the Levites were allowed, even *commanded* to play only cymbals, harps, and lyres. Only the priests were assigned to blow the trumpets, and only trumpets. All of that was to occur only while the burnt offering was being presented. Because only the temple worship specified the use of instruments, Jewish synagogues have never used them.

Therefore, it is inconsistent to claim Old Testament authority for mechanical instruments while ignoring the context in which those instruments were used in the temple worship. One must look to the New Testament instead and ask, "How did the early Christians worship?" The New Testament specifies that the music of the church is to be vocal music. Its silence on the instrument is a thundering silence. Instruments were available, *but the early church did not use them.*

In Ephesians 5:18–21, the command to "be filled with the Spirit," leads to participles that describe what Christians do who *are* filled with the Spirit. They are speaking ..., singing ..., making melody in the heart ..., giving thanks ..., and submitting to one another. The "instrument" or "organ" of music is the human heart, giving praise to God through the lips (cf. Hebrews 13:15). Mechanical instruments are not *necessary* or *expedient* in the carrying out of this teaching, nor are they *capable* of speaking, singing, etc. Also note Colossians 3:15–17.

Some have tried to claim New Testament authority for instruments in the use of the Greek term *psallo* in Ephesians

5:19. They have said that the term once meant to "pluck" a stringed instrument. If that were the case, *every* Christian would be required to pluck a stringed instrument in every worship assembly. In fact, the word *psallo* appears also in 1 Corinthians 14:15 and James 5:13, where only vocal expression is in view. The Septuagint (the Greek translation of the Hebrew Old Testament) also sometimes uses *psallo* in this purely vocal sense (Psalm 135:3, 138:1, 146:2).

The visions in Revelation depict harps and other items of Old Testament temple worship as symbols of heavenly realities. For example, bowls of incense represent the prayers of the saints. There are also golden lampstands, the temple itself, the altar of burnt offering, and the ark of the covenant. These items, including the harps, were never part of the early church's worship.

Historical Support for Vocal Music

"A cappella," referring today to unaccompanied vocal singing, is Latin, meaning "in the manner of the chapel/church." Singing without instruments is singing in the manner of the church.

Confirmation from Historians

- Lyman Coleman, a Presbyterian scholar, wrote, "Both the Jews in their temple service and the Greeks in their idol worship were accustomed to sing with the accompaniment of instrumental music. The converts to Christianity must have been familiar with this model of singing, but it is generally admitted that the primitive Christians

employed no instrumental music in their religious
worship".[1]

- Joseph Bingham, of the Church of England wrote,
  "Music in the Church is as ancient as the apostles;
  but instrumental music is not."[2]
- Hugo Leichtentritt wrote: "Only singing, however,
  and no playing of instruments, was permitted in
  the early Christian Church."[3]
- Frank Landon Humphreys wrote: "The early
  Christians discouraged all outward signs of
  excitement, and from the very beginning, in the
  music they used, reproduced the spirit of their
  religion — an outward quietude. All the music
  employed in their early services was vocal."[4]

Confirmation from Early Religious Leaders

- Clement of Alexandria (150–210 AD): "Leave the
  pipe to the shepherd, the flute to the men who are
  in fear of gods and intent on their idol
  worshipping. Such musical instruments must be
  excluded from our wineless feasts, for they are
  more suited for beasts and for the class of men that
  is least capable of reason than for men."[5] "The one
  instrument of peace, the word alone by which we
  honor God, is what we employ. We

---

1. *The Primitive Church*, 370–371.
2. *Antiquities of the Church*, 2:482.
3. *Music, History and Ideas*, 34.
4. *Evolution of Church Music*, 42.
5. Clement of Alexandria, *The Instructor*, The Fathers of the Church (Washington: Catholic University of America Press, 1954), 130.

no longer employ the ancient psaltery and trumpet, and timbrel, and flute."[6]

- Origen (325 AD): "For the unison song of the people of Christ is more pleasing to God than any musical instrument. Thereby in all the churches of God with one mind and heart, with unity and agreement in faith and worship, we offer to God a unison melody in our singing of Psalms."[7]

- Eusebius of Caesarea (260–340 AD): "… We render our hymn with a living psalterion and a living cithara with spiritual songs. The unison voices of Christians would be more acceptable to God than any musical instrument."[8]

- John Chrysostom (345–407 AD): "There is no need of lyre there, nor stretched strings nor plectrum, nor of musical skill, nor of any instruments. But if you choose, you will make yourself the lyre, putting to death the members of the flesh …"[9] "… in olden times they were thus led by these instruments because of the dullness of their understanding and their recent deliverance from idols. Just as God allowed animal sacrifices, so also He let them have these instruments, condescending to help their weakness."[10]

- Thomas Aquinas, a leading Catholic of his age (1250 AD): "Our church does not use musical

---

6. Clement of Alexandria, *Paedagogus* 2.4.

7. As quoted in *Restoration Quarterly* 1.1, (1957), 4.

8. *Commentary on Psalms* 91.2, 3.

9. *Exposition of Psalm 41,* Source *Readings in Music History,* ed. O. Strunk (New York: W. W. Norton, 1950), 70.

10. Chrysostom, on Ps. 150; *Patrologia Graeca* 55:494.

instruments, as harps and psalteries, to praise God withal, that she may not seem to Judaize."[11]

Confirmation from Religious Reformers

- John Calvin, influential in Presbyterian and Reformed churches: "Musical instruments in celebrating the praise of God would be no more suitable than the burning of incense, the lighting of lamps, the restoration of the other shadows of the law. The Papists, therefore, have foolishly borrowed this, as well as many other things, from the Jews."[12]
- John Wesley, influential in Wesleyan and Methodist churches: "I have no objection to instruments of music in our chapels, provided they are neither heard nor seen."[13]
- Adam Clarke, Methodist commentator (1762–1832 AD): "Music as a science, I esteem and admire; but instruments of music in the house of God I abominate and abhor. This is the abuse of music; and here I register my protest against all such corruptions in the worship of the Author of Christianity."[14]
- Martin Luther called the organ "an ensign of Baal."[15]
- Charles H. Spurgeon, 19th-century Baptist preacher in London: "Israel was a school, and used childish things to help her to learn, but in these

---

11. As quoted in *McClintock and Strong's Encyclopedia*, 7.739.
12. *John Calvin's Commentary*, Thirty-third Psalm.
13. As quoted in *Clarke's Commentary*, 4.686.
14. *Clarke's Commentary*, 4.686.
15. *McClintock & Strong's Encyclopedia of Music*, 7.762.

days, when Jesus gives us spiritual food, one can make melody without strings and pipes ... We do not need them. They would hinder rather than help our praise. Sing unto Him. This is the sweetest and best music. No instrument like human voice ... We might as well pray by machinery as praise by it."

- Alexander Campbell, 19th-century restorationist: "But I presume, to all spiritually-minded Christians, such aids [as instrumental music] would be as a cow bell in a concert."[16]

Practical Support for Vocal Music

The introduction of instruments, without biblical warrant, has created division and various other problems. Many groups have divided still further over which "traditional" or "contemporary" instruments they personally prefer. Bands and music have been developed to attract the popular culture by imitating the world's favorite secular genres. Sometimes the message seems to be, "Come to our church. We have the best music. We have a celebrity coming to perform or lead our worship this Sunday!" Some modern church assemblies leave the impression that entertainment has taken priority over edification. By contrast, how refreshing it is to return to the fresh waters of biblical, faithful, fervent, heart-felt congregational singing of praise to God!

---

16. *Millennial Harbinger* 4.1 (September 1851), 581–582.

Questions for Thought and Discussion

1. Read Psalms 115–18, the hymns that first-century Jews often sang to conclude the Passover.
2. Read Acts 16:20–30. What is most impressive to you about Paul's and Silas's singing?
3. In your opinion, why did they not need an organ, an orchestra, or a band?
4. Who bears the burden of proof, those who add such instruments or those who do not?
5. What did Jesus say about the Jewish, temple-centered worship of the Old Testament?
6. Describe what that temple-based system required, based on 2 Chronicles 29:20–36.
7. Explain why *psallo* in the New Testament era did not denote the use of musical instruments.
8. What "organ" or "instrument" has God specified for use in the church's worship?
9. What if instruments feel more worshipful to man or attract more people in the world?
10. What about the mention of harps, the temple, the ark, altars, and incense in Revelation?
11. What did "a cappella" originally mean, and why is that so significant?
12. What did John Calvin, Martin Luther, John Wesley, and Charles Spurgeon understand about singing as worship?
13. Lacking clear New Testament authority, why would man add organs and bands?
14. What practical problems and divisions have resulted from the introduction of instruments?

Chapter 16
Fresh Waters: Organization
Acts 20:17–38

At first, matters of church government may seem to be of minor importance. After all, why shouldn't people choose whatever system they think will work best? However, think about that for a moment. God's New Testament design, if it had been followed, would have prevented the large-scale departures and divisions that have occurred in the religious world throughout history. No individual or group would have taken charge of multiple congregations. No denominations would have formed. No independent, single-pastor, community-driven groups would have emerged. No man-made councils, creeds, confessions, dogmas, or traditions would have ever formed.

Respecting the Lord's design for the government of the church really means respecting Christ Himself. This is no trivial discussion, but a Christ-centered presentation in an effort to understand, restore, and implement His will for the church. For these reasons and more, the organization of the church is much more than just the nuts and bolts of some enterprise. It is, in fact, a spiritual matter; it is a biblical matter. And that makes it vitally important.

The Universal, Permanent Head of the Church

Jesus Christ is the one Head of His one church, its only source of authority and the only object of its glory. Jesus Christ established the church. He bought her, He owns her, and He rules her. The Word of God declares regarding Him,

> He is the image of the invisible God, the firstborn over all creation. For by Him all things were created that are in heaven and that are on earth, visible and invisible, whether thrones or dominions or principalities or powers. All things were created through Him and for Him. And He is before all things, and in Him all things consist. And He is the head of the body, the church, who is the beginning, the firstborn from the dead, that in all things He may have the preeminence (Colossians 1:15–18).

See also Ephesians 1:10, 22; 4:15; 5:23.

The very idea of a rival head, or even a representative earthly head of the church, would have been unthinkable in the first century. There was only one body, with only one Head.

The First-Century, Transitional Leaders of the Church

During His earthly ministry, the Lord appointed twelve men to be His apostles, "ones sent" or "missionaries" (Mark 3:13–19). They were His constant companions. He trained them during His earthly ministry. He sent them two-by-two into various cities ahead of His own arrival. He authorized them to carry out His instructions as the Holy Spirit would speak through them (Matthew 10:19–20) and to continue His mission after His departure.

On the night before He died, Jesus said to these apostles

regarding this matter, "... he who receives whomever I send receives Me; and he who receives Me receives Him who sent Me" (John 13:20). He went on to say that the Helper, the Holy Spirit, would come in His name, teach them all things, and remind them of all that He had said (John 14:26). The Spirit would guide them into all truth. He will take what was Christ and declare it to them (John 16:13–14).

After His resurrection, He told these apostles,

> " ... As the Father has sent Me, I also send you." Then He breathed on them and said, "Receive the Holy Spirit. If you forgive the sins of any, they are forgiven them; if you retain the sins of any, they are retained" (John 20:21–23).

Their authority was not their own. They were merely human agents and mouthpieces for the Lord. Neither Peter nor any other was to be the pope or "papa" of the church. These men would be directed by the Spirit to bind or loose on earth that which had already been bound or loosed in heaven (Matthew 16:18–19, 18:18; NASB). On the Day of Pentecost, the Holy Spirit came to enable the apostles to preach the gospel; thus, Christ established the church (Acts 2). By preaching heaven's message, Peter used the "keys of the kingdom" as God's agent to offer salvation. All of God's truth would then be revealed through the apostles and recorded in the New Testament (1 Corinthians 2:6–13, 14:37; 2 Corinthians 13:10; Ephesians 3:3–6; 1 Thessalonians 2:13).

In this way the church was "built on the foundation of (laid by) the apostles and prophets, with Christ Jesus himself as the chief cornerstone" (Ephesians 2:20). Paul said: "For no one can lay any foundation other than the one already laid, which is Jesus Christ" (1 Corinthians 3:11). Peter himself declared that Jesus Christ, not Peter himself, was the foundation rock of the church (1 Peter 2:4–8). So, Christ built His church, not on any man, but on Himself through men.

The Ongoing, Local Leaders of the Churches

The timeframe for apostles for the church worldwide had to end since only a personal eyewitness of Christ was qualified to become an apostle (Acts 1:21–22). So, under Christ's authority, those who spread the gospel "appointed elders in every church" (Acts 14:23). God's design was to establish a plurality of male leaders to oversee and pastor (shepherd) each individual congregation. The Jerusalem church had such elders, for example (Acts 11:30).

During the transitional period, the apostles and these elders met together and conferred regarding God's will for the church at large (Acts 15:1–6, 22, 23; 16:4). However, once the apostles died, each individual congregation would be led independently by its own local elders.

Deacons were specialized servants who would involve others in service. Quite possibly, the seven men chosen to care for the widows in Acts 6 served as deacons. God's plan was simple. For example, Paul wrote "... to all the saints in Christ Jesus who are in Philippi, including the overseers and deacons" (Philippians 1:1). The apostles gave inspired instructions regarding the qualities of these overseers and deacons (See 1 Timothy 3:1–7, Titus 1:5–9, and 1 Peter 5:1–4).

As stated before, the New Testament says nothing about human councils, conventions, dioceses, or any leadership structure above the local congregation. The idea of a denominational-style hierarchy was completely unknown in the first-century church.

The apostle Paul met with the local leaders of the church in Ephesus. He prepared them for the ongoing leadership that they would continue to exercise after his departure. As one carefully reads what he told them in Acts 20:17–38, one sees three significant terms that described them.

> [Paul] called the *elders* of the [Ephesian] church and said ... "Be on guard for yourselves and for all the flock, among which the Holy Spirit has made you *overseers*, to *shepherd* the church of God which He purchased with His own blood" (Acts 20:17, 28).

These three words are used interchangeably in the New Testament to describe the same group of male church leaders in a local congregation, indicating three aspects of their responsibility.

Elders—First, they are "elders." The Greek word, *presbyteros,* is a comparative term meaning "older men." It signifies maturity, wisdom, and delegated decision-making authority under Christ. In Old Testament times, each city's elders would meet at the city gate, hear cases, and execute God's will (for example, Deuteronomy 21:1–9). The gospels mention the decision-making leadership of Jewish elders in Jerusalem in Jesus's time (Matthew 16:21, 21:23, 27:1).

Elders who led or ruled wisely were to be honored and even compensated. They were to be protected from unconfirmed criticism and accusations. However, elders who sinned were to be rebuked publicly to warn others (1 Timothy 5:17–20).

Overseers—Second, Paul said that the Holy Spirit had made these same men, these elders, to be "overseers." The Greek word, *episkopos,* indicates the supervisory, administrative, and organizational responsibility of these men. In particular, they were to "watch over" the church so that false teachers could not ravage it like wolves attacking defenseless sheep. Because these men were appointed ultimately by the Holy Spirit Himself, they should take their work very seriously. This term *episkopos* also appears in Philippians 1:1, 1 Timothy 3:1–2, Titus 1:7, 1 Peter 5:2. Scripture calls Jesus Christ Himself "the Overseer of your souls" (1 Peter 2:25).

Hebrews 13:17, while not using the term overseer, says that local church leaders *keep watch over you* as men who must give an account. Christians are told to obey them and submit to their authority. As a result, the work of these overseers would be a joy and not a burden, as a blessing and advantage to the disciples that they would lead.

As church history developed, the term "bishop" came to be used to refer to *just one man* who had the oversight of *an entire congregation or a group of congregations* (a diocese). This is the "episcopal" form of leadership. It does not have this meaning in the New Testament but refers rather to one "overseer" among a group of overseers who lead a single congregation.

Shepherds or Pastors—Third, the shepherding or pastoral role would involve counseling, nurturing, protecting, correcting, and leading (Psalm 23, Ezekiel 34:1–6, Luke 15:3–7, John 10:1–18). Shepherds would personally attend to the needs of individuals, whether they were idle, timid, or weak. They were to warn, teach, encourage, admonish, and rebuke (1 Thessalonians 5:12–15). They would visit and pray for the sick, that they might be healed (James 5:13–18).

Many today use "pastors" to refer to individual preachers or ministers rather than to the plural group of leaders also known as elders and overseers. Timothy and Titus were never told to pastor or shepherd churches but rather to identify others who would do so. Though a single man like Paul served as a preacher, only married men with children could be overseers and pastor the local church (1 Timothy 3:1–7, Titus 1:5–9). Non-pastor preachers were to preach the Word, do the work of an evangelist (gospel proclaimer), and fulfill their ministry (2 Timothy 4:1–5).

Confirmation—Peter noted these same three terms and functions. He wrote as a fellow elder (not as a pope or the church's earthly "Holy Father") to the other *elders* of the churches, telling them to *shepherd* God's flock, serving as *overseers* (1 Peter 5:1–2).

Confusion and Clarity

In New Testament times there were no popes, cardinals, monsignors, archbishops, monks, nuns, reverends, or senior pastors. There was no pyramid or denominational hierarchy. No churches were named after a "presbyterian," "episcopalian," or "congregational" style of government. Yet a denomination today, for example, may have its own Constitution, General Conference, Council of Bishops, Judicial Council, and High Court. There are legal and financial barriers when churches try to leave their denomination over changing moral and doctrinal beliefs. Even a cursory online search for "church government" produces an overwhelming amount of confusing information.

Those who seek to return to fresh waters do not offer a better man-made system or a superior denomination. They refuse to do so! They must approach this matter, as well as all other matters, with an attitude of humility and a passionate desire to do God's things in God's ways, according to God's pattern, and with a view to God's glory. They seek to go back, way back, before today's confusion began, and obey that which God gave the church of Jesus Christ.

Questions for Thought and Discussion

1. Why is the matter of church leadership and organization not minor or trivial?

2. Why does such a study honor Christ, rather than detract from Him?

3. What scriptures emphasize the unique, sovereign, unrivaled role of Christ as the church's head?

4. What does the New Testament teach about the apostles' delegated, inspired authority?

5. Why was the apostleship necessarily of limited duration?

6. "The apostles played a foundational role, but the church's foundation is Christ." Discuss.

7. How might the widows' needs in Acts 6 illustrate the role of deacons as specialized servants?

8. Discuss Paul's message to the elders from Ephesus regarding leadership (Acts 20:17–38).

9. What does the term "elder" mean, and what leadership functions does it signify?

10. What does the term "overseer" mean, and what leadership functions does it signify?

11. What does the term "shepherd" mean, and what leadership functions does it signify?

12. How has the term "pastor" been misunderstood and misapplied in the religious world?

13. Research the leadership structure of any modern denomination and summarize it.

Chapter 17
Fresh Waters: Non-Denominationalism
Acts 2:36–47

J esus Christ always spoke of the church that He would establish as a single community. He called it "one flock" (John 10:16), "My church" (Matthew 16:18), and "the church" (Matthew 18:17). He used images such as one field (Matthew 13:24–30), one mustard tree (Matthew 13:31–32), and one fishing net (Matthew 13:47–52) to describe His one kingdom. The night before He died, He prayed "that all of [My followers] may be one, Father, just as you are in me and I am in you ... so that the world may believe" (John 17:20–23).

One Church

Scripture emphasizes the oneness of the church and urges Christians to maintain that unity with great zeal and passion.

> Make every effort to keep the unity of the Spirit through the bond of peace. There is one body and one Spirit—just as you were called to one hope when you were called—one Lord, one faith, one baptism; one God and Father of all, who is over all and through all and in all (Ephesians 4:3–6).

On the other side of the coin, the New Testament denounces division.

> I appeal to you, brothers, in the name of our Lord Jesus Christ, that all of you agree with one another so that there may be no divisions among you and that you may be perfectly united in mind and thought .... One of you says, "I follow Paul," another, "I follow Apollos," another, "I follow Cephas," still another, "I follow Christ." Is Christ divided? Was Paul crucified for you? Were you baptized into the name of Paul (1 Corinthians 1:10–13)?

Divisions: Names and Creeds

Sadly however, the record of history stands in stark contrast to Jesus's prayer and the apostles' inspired teachings. Hundreds of groups have formed, divided both by names and creeds, all claiming to be followers of Christ. Some deny the deity of Christ, some insist that Saturday is the day of worship, some teach that baptism is not essential to salvation, some pray to Mary and various "saints," some claim to have additional revelation beyond the Bible, some ordain women and homosexuals to church leadership, and so forth. Further subdivisions have created more branches in the denominational tree that are almost too many to count.

Some religious groups wear names that distinguish them from others and indicate their unique identity. A name may highlight the group's scope. For example, "Catholic" means "universal;" "Southern" points to a section of the U.S. It may suggest a style of government. For example, "Episcopalian" means "bishop-style," while "Presbyterian" means "elder-style." It may highlight a specific practice, such as "Baptist" or "Seventh-Day Adventist," or a theological view, such as "Reformed" or "Pentecostal."

It may further distinguish itself from others within the
same branch. For example, "Southern Baptists," "Independent
Baptists," "Primitive Baptists," "Missionary Baptists," and
"Freewill Baptists" are all separate fellowships. The "Presbyterian Church U.S.A." is distinct in belief and practice from
the "Orthodox Presbyterian Church." The "Lutheran Church
(Missouri Synod)" is not in fellowship with other Lutherans.
A group's name may reflect the influence of a particular
leader, such as "Lutheran" or "Wesleyan." It may describe a
restricted ethnic complexion, such as "African Methodist
Episcopal."

To complicate matters further, some denominations have
applied to themselves *as distinct denominations* the descriptive
phrases that the New Testament uses to describe *the entire
church*. For example, "church of God" is a biblical description
(Acts 20:28; 1 Corinthians 1:2, 10:32, 11:22, 15:9; 2 Corinthians
1:1; Galatians 1:9) for all of God's people. However, if one says
today, "I belong to the church of God," others may think he
refers to a "Church of God" denomination.

"Community churches" today reflect a non-affiliated
stance, even independent of each other. These names may
single out biblical truths (sadly, to the exclusion of other
equally-precious truths) such as grace, faith, love, or fellowship. Or their names may have no Bible connection at all,
such as Gateway, Northwood, Keystone, Milestone, Compass,
or Venture.

The Non-Denominational Dilemma

All of this poses a dilemma for those committed to the
restoration of New Testament Christianity, who claim no
membership in anything other than the one church described
in Scripture. *How shall they identify themselves?* They must
somehow communicate to a denominational world, "We are

Christians, nothing else. We belong to the body of Christ. We have no denomination. We believe that the very idea of religious division is sinful because it contradicts the unity for which Jesus Christ prayed and gave His life."

Yet others may ask, "What *kind* of Christians?" When they mention the church or the body of Christ, people may ask, "Which *type* of church?" If they use biblical phrases like "disciples of Christ," "the church of God," or "the churches of Christ," others may *hear* "X denomination." If they simply say, "I belong to *the church*," they may appear arrogant, ignorant, or even evasive.

In Acts 2, about 3,000 people accepted the gospel message and were baptized. The Lord "added" them to the church, nothing more. In the first century, one of these 3,000 might have answered regarding his new faith, "I belong to the church." Or, "I am a Christian, a disciple of Christ." Or, "I follow the Way." Or, "I am a member of Christ's church, the household of God, the body of Christ, the churches of Christ, or the church of God." All of these are biblical descriptions. None of these would have indicated any particular sect or denomination, for of course, these were unknown to the early believers. They all belonged to the one church that Christ built. Today, however, it is difficult to communicate the non-denominational nature of "the church."

An Illustration

G. C. Brewer illustrated the dilemma this way. He supposed that he had a great heap of cards. Some were stamped with numbers 2, 4, 6, 8, etc. Many were unstamped. He imagined trying to separate the cards and classify them. He put the 2s in one stack, the 4s in another, and the unstamped cards in another. A card from the stack of 8s arose and said to the unstamped cards, "You claim to be unstamped and non-denominational, yet you are bunched, stacked, and classified as much as any of us!" Then a card from the nondescript bunch vehemently replied: "We are not classified. We have no denomination. We are just cards!"

Brewer noted that these were forced to be in a stack to themselves because the others were separated into stacks and left them alone. They were "classified" by reason of the fact that they were "unclassified." It was not their purpose to be a distinct division of cards. They thought all cards ought to be just cards and to be stacked together in one stack, but the other cards were all stamped with different distinguishing figures. Brewer said:

> You can all see the application .... We are forced to be a sepa-
> rate body of people because we are undenominational,
> because we will not have put on us the party names, marks,
> and brands of the different denominations. We want the
> fellowship of all of God's people, and we will affiliate with
> anybody in anything the Bible sanctions, but we cannot have
> the fellowship of our denominational brethren without going
> into their peculiar and separate denominations .... Our
> purposes and work as a body of Christians - undenomina-
> tional Christians, simply Christians, Christians only—make
> it necessary for us to labor apart from the denominations ....
> 1

A Distinctive Call to Unity

Ironically this Restoration Plea, which calls for the nonde-nominational, Bible-based *unity* of all believers in Christ, inevitably results in *division*, though it does not *cause* division. It insists that any person, anywhere and anytime, may hear the gospel of Christ, respond to it biblically, and become a Christian. The Lord adds him or her to His church, the body of Christ, not to any man-made denomination. This person may worship, fellowship, and serve with others who share this pure biblical faith. These Christians may (and must) remain just that, never adding man-made beliefs, practices, or a man-made denominational creed or hierarchy.

They welcome as Christians all others who obey the gospel as the New Testament teaches and who wish to worship and serve according to the New Testament pattern. They may claim all the biblical descriptions applied to the church: church of God, churches of Christ, household of faith, bride of Christ, body of Christ, etc. They refuse the unbiblical changes discussed previously.

Doing these things does not make this group of Christians and congregations a denomination, though they will be a separate, distinct people. Deliberately choosing to come out of the denominations and be nothing but Christians, they are not able to worship with or fully fellowship those who have changed important elements of New Testament teaching. Their appeal to a divided, sectarian religious world is, "Abandon all denominational names and creeds and return to the faith and practice of the early church. Together, let's just be Christians!"

Churches of Christ

The designation "churches of Christ" (Romans 16:16) is biblical and helpful in identifying many who share this plea; it is not to be used in a denominational sense. If one says, "I'm Church of Christ. I was baptized by a Church of Christ minister, I attended a Church of Christ school," etc., he or she does not clearly convey or perhaps understand the Bible's non-sectarian teaching.

One might say instead, "I am a Christian. I have no denominational affiliation. I am trying to believe, practice, and obey nothing but the teaching of Christ and the apostles. I am part of a congregation of Christians that holds this same view. We welcome all others who follow Christ biblically. We are Christ's disciples, God's church, the body and bride of Christ, etc. There are many such congregations, often known as churches of Christ. We plead for the unity of all who would follow Christ, and we believe that such unity is possible through biblical restoration, that is, a return to nothing but the teaching of Scripture."

The phrase "church of Christ" is not copyrighted. Any group, regardless of their beliefs, can put that phrase on a sign! So, it remains vital to explore not only a group's advertised name, but also its beliefs, teachings, and practices in the light of the New Testament. When all is said and done, "... the solid foundation of God stands, having this seal: 'The Lord knows those who are His,' and, 'Let everyone who names the name of Christ depart from iniquity'" (2 Timothy 2:19).

Questions for Thought and Discussion

1. How important was the unity of the church to Christ Himself? What did He say about it?
2. In light of His teaching, why is the very idea of denominations wrong, even sinful?
3. In Ephesians 4:3–6 we find seven "ones." Name them. Why are they important?
4. Why must we "make every effort to maintain unity?" Why is unity difficult to maintain?
5. How did some of today's denominations and community churches choose their names?
6. Read Revelation 2–3. Did some churches, by changing their teaching and practices, cease to be

faithful to Christ? What would be necessary before He would accept them again?

7. What has caused religious division? Are the churches of Christ responsible for it?

8. Discuss the "great heap of cards" and the dilemma of the non-sectarian Restoration Plea.

9. To what church does the Lord add every person who obeys the gospel as in Acts 2?

10. Could any group anywhere follow only the New Testament pattern and be just Christians?

11. What idea might the statement, "I'm Church of Christ," convey to other people?

12. How can a Christian answer the question, "What church do you belong to?"

13. How can we draw others, not to follow us or "our church," but to pursue the Restoration Plea?

---

[1] G. C. Brewer, *Foundation Facts and Primary Principles*, 1949, p. 61.

Chapter 18
Fresh Waters: Balance
Matthew 23:1–38

Jesus Christ struck a perfect balance in His teaching and ministry. He put vital elements of faith and obedience into a beautiful, clear, and harmonious perspective. For example, He taught radical commitment to God (Luke 14:25–35), yet He also told His followers to "Give to Caesar what is Caesar's" (Matthew 22:15–22). His message about life after death included both a central focus on God and a primary focus on doctrine regarding the resurrection (Matthew 22:23–33). He did not play the two against each other or emphasize the one to the neglect of the other. When asked about the greatest commandment, He emphasized the priority of inward love for God and neighbor, and at the same time, He stressed the necessity of observing God's outward rules that would express that love (Matthew 22:34–40). He said that the latter "hung upon" the former.

He clarified His identity as the one that David called "Lord," and yet He did so by a careful explanation of Scripture (Matthew 22:41–45). He taught the sovereignty of God as His disciples' unique Father, and He also told His disciples, based on this fact, "... do not call anyone on earth 'father'"

(Matthew 23:9). He rebuked the Pharisees for neglecting justice, mercy, and faithfulness, which He called "the more important matters of the law," but He also commended them for lesser things like giving their tithe of tiny garden plants (Matthew 23:23).

Goal: Keeping the Balance

The apostles, filled with the Word of Christ and led by the Spirit of Christ, carefully maintained the balance and perspective of their Master in their preaching and writing. The goal of restoration must always be for Christians both to *rediscover* the various elements of New Testament faith and practice and also to *reposition* these elements in the balanced framework that Jesus Christ and the apostles set forth originally. Christians must see "as of first importance" what the apostles saw: that Christ died, was buried, was raised, and appeared (1 Corinthians 15:1–5). From that reference point, they seek to recognize every element of biblical truth in its proper place.

The previous chapters in this series have approached restoration principles from this standpoint. They have shown that Christians are committed to biblical teaching on every subject *just because of their wholehearted commitment to the person and work of Christ.* The Restoration Plea itself is a plea for Jesus Christ to have His way in the church. The emphasis on biblical authority is Christ's emphasis. He Himself (as well as the apostles and New Testament writers) used direct statements, examples, and implications to explain what the Scriptures command, what they allow, and what they prohibit. It was He who rejected human traditions that made changes or substitutions regarding the Father's will.

Christ Himself distinguished the Old Testament administration from that of the New. He applied the principle of exclusion, showing that God's specifying what He wanted excluded additions and substitutions. He respected Scripture's silence. He allowed expedients, practical means of doing what God had commanded. He related grace, faith, and obedience to each other. He taught the necessity of baptism, involving both water and the Spirit. He set forth the Lord's Supper. He laid the groundwork for worshipping with the heart (not mechanical instruments) and organizing the church with a plurality of male spiritual leaders. He then further revealed these matters by giving His Spirit to lead the apostles "into all the truth" (John 16:13).

Not Either/Or, but Rather Both/And

So, Christians are not asked or forced to choose between "just loving Jesus" and "observing all that Jesus commanded." They may have both the centrality of the cross and the necessity of baptism in water, both worship from the heart and worship without a mechanical aid. They must keep both the *purpose* of the Lord's Supper (remembering the cross and re-examining their hearts) and the *pattern* of the Lord's Supper (unleavened bread and the fruit of the vine on the first day of every week). They may keep Christ as the "Chief Shepherd" while also insisting that local shepherds (or elders) meet the specific qualifications given in Scripture (1 Peter 5:1–4).

They are not forced to choose between "being spiritual" and "being scriptural." They are not caught in the false dilemma between "the person of Christ" and "the pattern of Christ," between "the man" and "the plan," between Jesus as their personal Savior and the church as His body in which they serve. They accept both love and law, both spirit and letter, both inward and outward, both grace and obedience, and both God's sovereignty and human responsibility. They may (and must) restore the outward without sacrificing the inward.

Some people have raised questions that set up apparent but invalid conflicts regarding Christian faith and practice. To each question, those who follow Christ must avoid the trap of taking only one side and must seek the balance of Jesus Christ and Scripture. These are a few of them.

- *Is the Bible a book of rules, or is it a love letter from God?*
- *Should we look for a pattern to restore, or a person to worship?*
- *Is Christianity about specific doctrines, or is it about Christ?*
- *Shall we restore just the doctrines and practices that we on our own decide are related to 'salvation issues,' or shall we seek to restore every element of apostolic teaching?*
- *Since we are not saved by our perfect understanding and performance, shall we minimize the importance of seeking to understand and perform as best we can, by the grace of God?*
- *Since no Christian or congregation is perfect and without sin, shall we just accept all denominational creeds and varieties as equally imperfect yet valid?*

In answering each of these questions, Christians must avoid a false "either/or" dichotomy, when the Scriptures present a "both/and" perspective. In addition, the church must seek to avoid both an overly restrictive view and an overly liberal view regarding biblical authority and Christian practice. These two extremes have affected and divided people within the religious world, as well as those within the restoration movement.

Imbalance—Binding What God Has Not Bound

Imagine that a company's CEO instructs his vice president to involve all his workers in preparing a financial report, to be on his desk by the following Tuesday morning. The vice president tells his subordinates that, in order to keep their jobs, they must follow very restrictive methods, which the CEO did not stipulate. They must use only 20-pound paper. They are forbidden to use certain of the company's photocopiers. They may not collaborate with each other on the project. They must not provide childcare on the premises. They must work on the report only from 9:00 until 11:00 a.m. They may not eat anywhere in the building or work in age-related groups.

The vice president says all this out of a sincere desire to do what the CEO instructed, but he overly restricts his workers and actually opposes choices that the CEO would have allowed. As a result, he becomes known as "anti" because many of his views appear negative. He may describe himself as "conservative," but he will be seen by some others as "restrictive."

In a similar way, some have sought to restrict the church's faith and practice in ways that God has not restricted them. Or they may attempt to set limits where God has allowed flexibility. Their constraints often result from their prior teaching and upbringing, their tender conscience, and their sincere desire to uphold biblical authority and silence. The Bible certainly emphasizes care and respect for others' consciences (Romans 14:1–23). Several questions come to mind.

What about age-based Bible classes or literature? May we have a church building? May such a building include an annex for shared meals, benevolence projects, or social events? May congregations cooperate financially in a shared benevolence or mission effort? May funds from the church treasury be spent on training preachers in a school designed for that purpose? May church funds be used to help non-Christians or just the saints? How are we to care for widows and orphans? Does the "one cup" or the "one loaf" of 1 Corinthians 10:16–17 require that the entire church drink from the same vessel or break off a piece of bread from the same loaf?

In my experience with those who hold more restrictive views than I do, I have found it helpful to ask and listen rather than to assume and prejudge. I admit to inconsistencies in my own thinking, and I try to learn how and why others think differently. From what scriptures do they draw what they consider to be necessary inferences? Are these genuinely biblical issues or are they more matters of tradition and preference?

When we served in the Philadelphia area, a brother came to us whose conscience prohibited him from eating with us in a separate area inside the church building. He asked if he could be part of the congregation in worship and work but excuse himself from events that involved meals. Of course! This arrangement was agreeable to all. We respected and appreciated his conscience.

Imbalance—Loosening What God Has Bound

Imagine (using the previous illustration) that the vice president tells his subordinates that the CEO loves them and has a few suggestions. They should feel good about themselves and their boss, and they should show their appreciation and commitment in some appropriate way. The VP mentions a financial report as a possibility, and he suggests a Tuesday deadline as a good option, but he opens the way to various alternatives. He recommends but does not require that all employees participate. Though he may also be sincere, he is violating his CEO's directions by not clearly stating his requirements. He is loosening what his boss has bound.

Perhaps a church accepts into membership those who have not been baptized into Christ for the forgiveness of sins. Another adds mechanical musical instruments and multiple services to accommodate the members' musical preferences. Some "traditional" services may still be a cappella or add an organ, while more "contemporary" services may employ a choir, an orchestra, or a full band with exotic lighting and other special effects. Another encourages women to read scripture, offer prayer, and even preach in the mixed worship assembly. Another church may emphasize grace, love, and heaven, while appearing to minimize sin, wrath, judgment, and hell.

Again, it's wise first to dialogue, ask, and listen. Where, if at all, do the "looseners" find biblical authority for their beliefs and practices? Why veer away from the safest course? After all, the Lord has given specific instructions regarding salvation, the purpose of baptism, elements of worship, the content of preaching, the permanence of marriage, the spiritual leadership of men, the call to non-denominational unity, and other aspects of biblical Christianity. To weaken what God has made clear, or to remain silent where God has spoken, is to violate His will.

Questions for Thought and Discussion

1. Give additional examples of the balance that Jesus exhibited in His ministry.
2. How did Jesus avoid being a Pharisee, while still insisting on biblical standards?
3. Some say, "Give me the Person, not some pattern!" How would you respond?

4. Why would some people elevate Jesus's own teaching, but take Paul less seriously?

5. How can we be both *spiritual* and *scriptural*, preserving both *form* and *function*?

6. Discuss the "either/or" conflicting questions and respond to them with biblical balance.

7. Why dare we not let our admission of imperfection keep us from seeking to overcome it?

8. Why must we not allow so-called "salvation issues" to minimize "obedience issues"?

9. What is one way that a vice president might violate his CEO's directions?

10. What other way might a vice president violate his CEO's directions?

11. Why is it so important that we ask and listen rather than assume and prejudge?

12. How can we respect tender consciences without becoming overly restrictive?

13. How might "looseners" try to justify adding female preachers and even elders?

Chapter 19
Fresh Waters: Assessment
Philippians 3:7–16

I feel a great sense of accomplishment when I hear the words, "You have arrived!" Unfortunately, it is only the GPS in my phone that ever tells me that! The Christian life is a journey that is not completed until we get to be at home with the Lord. So it is with the church. In a very real sense, much of the New Testament church's faith and practice has been restored. Yet it is equally true that further restoration is urgently needed. The church is both restored and restoring.

When Paul the apostle evaluated his faith, his knowledge, and his accomplishments, he was stunningly transparent. He knew Christ, and yet he still yearned to come to know Christ. He had suffered much for Christ, but he still longed to be conformed to His death. Even after he had made so much progress in his sacrifice, service, and God-given mission, he wrote,

> Not that I have already attained, or am already perfected; but I press on, that I may lay hold of that for which Christ Jesus has also laid hold of me. Brethren, I do not count myself to have apprehended; but one thing I do, forgetting

those things which are behind and reaching forward to those things which are ahead, I press toward the goal for the prize of the upward call of God in Christ Jesus (Philippians 3:12–14).

He went on to urge mature brethren to adopt the same mindset.

In other words, this great man of God acknowledged that he had not yet arrived. There were more miles to be run and more deeds to be done. As Christians today seek to identify with the one church of Christ described in the Bible, we must acknowledge both how far God has brought us and also how eager we are to continue the journey, back to where fresh waters flow.

Biblical teaching has not changed, yet every generation must be taught afresh. Each disciple must be trained anew in the heart and the message of Jesus Christ. Today's church and then today's world must hear the unchanging gospel in its purest form.

Back to the Spring

The Restoration Plea calls every believer back to the mountain, back to the fresh spring water of Christian faith and practice that originated in the New Testament. The trip may be costly and tiring. It may require radical thinking and effort. It may challenge the additives that well-meaning people have poured into the water through the years. However, it will be worth the effort.

Our goal must not be to restore the church to some previous Reformation or Restoration Movement, whether dating back to the 1500s in Europe, the 1800s in Scotland and America, or to any other time and place since Acts 2. The pattern for the church's faith and practice was not created by any human being or group dating later than the first century. Rather we seek what true restorationists have always sought —the clear, simple, original biblical source.

Some important elements of New Testament faith and practice *have been restored* in many congregations. These include matters related to baptism, the weekly observance of the Lord's Supper, the organization of local congregations with elders, deacons, and evangelists, and so forth. In some areas, Christians may humbly and truthfully say, "We have returned to the spring."

At the same time, believers in Christ are *still restoring* genuine faith and practice. They determine to keep going back to the original spring again and again. They never feel that they have fully arrived or perfectly attained the will of God. Man's tendency is to depart from God's plan, to substitute, add to, or subtract from His design. The studies in this book overwhelmingly confirm this fact. Mature Christians recognize this truth and are therefore always on guard against apostasy and always diligent to continue seeking to restore the ancient faith according to God's pattern.

Areas of Further Restoration

I personally recognize my own continuing need to "keep growing in the grace and knowledge of our Lord and Savior Jesus Christ" (2 Peter 3:18). As I observe my own life, as well as other Christians and congregations that I have known, I sense an ongoing need to address various matters more fervently. I note these, not as an indictment, but rather as a challenge, first of all to myself.

Love for God

The greatest command of all is to love God with all of

one's heart, soul, mind, and strength (Mark 12:30). Who can say, "I have fully accomplished this?" Certainly not I! Revival and restoration begin and continue only with a fever-pitch craving to know God—His heart, His Word, and His will. As Jesus said, it is those who "hunger and thirst for right-eousness" who will be filled (Matthew 5:6). When man wants the Word of God more than he wants bread, God will cause his cup to overflow (Deuteronomy 8:3; Matthew 4:4; Psalm 19:10, 23:5).

Hunger for God leads one from just "giving as commanded" to giving beyond his ability because he has first given himself to the Lord (2 Corinthians 8:1–5). Hunger for God drives one to pray fervently into the night. Hunger for God causes one to sing, certainly without mechanical instru-ments, but also with passionate zeal (Acts 16:25). Hunger for God motivates disciples to think on things above rather than earthly things and to act accordingly (Colossians 3:1–4).

Love for Each Other

The second greatest command, which reflects that first love for God, is to love one's neighbor as one loves himself (Mark 12:31). Jesus illustrated that truth by describing a Samaritan who went out of his way to care for a Jew who had been left on the side of the road to die (Luke 10:25–37). The New Testament calls Christians to lay down our lives for each other as Christ did for us and, therefore, share our posses-sions with each other (1 John 3:16f, cf. Acts 4:32–35).

We are to bear one another's burdens (Galatians 6:2), exhort one another daily (Hebrews 3:13), and regard one another as more important than ourselves (Philippians 2:3). Each Christian has received a gift, which he or she is to use to minister to one another (1 Peter 4:10).

The church is not a building or a mere assembly; it is

rather a living, growing organism. From Christ "the whole body, joined and knit together by what every joint supplies, according to the effective working by which every part does its share, causes growth of the body for the edifying of itself in love" (Ephesians 4:16, cf. Romans 12:3–8, 1 Corinthians 12:12–27).

God intends that each faithful member has a role to play, a job to do, in the local church body, as part of the family. Further restoration calls Christians to grow beyond regular participation in Bible study, worship, and observance of the Lord's Supper and to discover and use their God-given gifts for the good and the growth of the body.

Love for Souls

One who loves God and others cannot help but seek to save others. Jesus's marching orders, to go into all the world, preach the gospel, and make disciples, still stand today as the mission of every Christian and every congregation. He never called His people to be comfortable in the fold, but to seek the stray in the mountains. Christians cannot hire professionals to do our evangelizing any more than we can employ others to do our praying. As we sing, "We have heard the Macedonian call today," we must go to our Macedonia, whether that is across the street or across the world. Jesus causes those who follow Him to become fishers of men (Mark 1:17).

The lack of numerical growth in the church today has not resulted from the weakness of the message; cults multiply rapidly even though based on falsehood. Nor is there a deficiency of divine power. God still promises that, if Christians will plant and water, He will make it grow (1 Corinthians 3:6). Nor is the church stagnant due to a poor harvest field. Jesus said: "The harvest is plentiful, but the workers are few. Ask the Lord of the harvest, therefore, to send out workers into his harvest field" (Matthew 9:37–38). A church committed to further restoration is a church ruthlessly and restlessly devoted to saving people. Such a church lives and breathes evangelism.

Cultural Influence

Jesus said, "You are the salt of the earth ... the light of the world ..." (Matthew 5:13 16). The first-century Christians "turned the world upside down" (Acts 17:6). The church is not only to save the lost; the church is also to infiltrate, saturate, and flavor the world, as yeast works its way through dough (Matthew 13:33). Is the church changing the culture, or is the culture changing the church? If we imitate the culture regarding morality, modesty, and money, we need restoration. Imagine the impact that Christians can have in the marketplace, in the legal and political process, and in the local community. The salt must not be content to stay in the salt shaker!

Paul took God's message to the world's great cities, like Athens and Rome. Whether the issue is cloning, abortion, gambling, pornography, feminism, capital punishment, criminal rehabilitation, public education, or any one of a myriad of other matters, the church must seek a way to be heard and to influence public thought and behavior. To whatever degree the church retreats from the culture, the church needs restoration. If the culture refuses to change, let it not be because the church refused its call to be salt and light.

Religious Dialogue

Jesus often interacted with religious people with whom He had sharp disagreements; He never retreated. The church must follow in His steps (1 Peter 2:21). Over time, firm lines and thick walls have developed between religious people who actually have much in common. The folks on each side may have become entrenched, and they may reinforce their identity by constantly talking only with each other about how wrong the people are who are on the other side of the fence.

Dialogue through the fence holes gives way to monologue. Engagement and interaction turn to inward reflection and the "circling of the wagons." Exclusion and isolation become the accepted norm. Christians must realize that discussion with others does not mean endorsement of their beliefs. We must tear down walls and build bridges, starting with basic areas of common ground—God, the cross, the resurrection, and faith. We must not demean the sincerity of others but show respect to all. We must "speak the truth in love" (Ephesians 4:15). We must not be quarrelsome, but kind (2 Timothy 2:23–26), to reach as many as possible (1 Corinthians 9:19–23).

It is my prayer that the material in this book may be of help. First, we ourselves must seek and drink from the fresh waters of New Testament Christianity. Then, as we better understand the causes of today's religious confusion, may we engage others in a biblical, Christ-centered way.

Questions for Thought and Discussion

1. Why must we never say, "We have arrived! The first-century church has been restored"?
2. What did the apostle Paul acknowledge about his own faith and practice?
3. Why does this generation desperately and uniquely need to hear the Restoration Plea?
4. What is the greatest commandment of all, and why is it the key to all else?

5. How can we move beyond attendance to every-member, one-another involvement?

6. In what ways can Christians grow in our love for souls and our personal gospel outreach?

7. In what areas is American culture making the greatest (or least) impact on the church?

8. In what areas is the church making the greatest (or least) impact on American culture?

9. How can we "infiltrate, saturate, and flavor" our increasingly secular culture?

10. What inhibits Christians from talking with other religious people about the Restoration Plea?

11. How can Christians talk more effectively with our religious neighbors?

12. What other areas of further needed growth would you add to this chapter's partial list?

13. In what ways do you personally need further restoration to first-century Christianity?

Chapter 20
Fresh Waters: Reflections
1 Corinthians 2:1–5

T hank you for reading this second edition of *Where Fresh Waters Flow: the Restoration Plea.* As I conclude this writing, I can identify with Paul regarding several things he said and wrote. First, I note with you the admission and intention which he expressed to the Corinthians.

> And I, brethren, when I came to you, did not come with excellence of speech or of wisdom declaring to you the testimony of God. For I determined not to know anything among you except Jesus Christ and Him crucified. I was with you in weakness, in fear, and in much trembling. And my speech and my preaching were not with persuasive words of human wisdom, but in demonstration of the Spirit and of power, that your faith should not be in the wisdom of men but in the power of God (1 Corinthians 2:1–5).

Everything that we believe, say, or do as Christians must be centered and founded on Jesus Christ and the cross. We do not preach, teach, or write to draw others to ourselves but to Him. We may lack "excellence of speech or of wisdom" as we present the wonderful truths of the gospel. We may be weak and fearful; we may even tremble, as Paul did! We may lack "persuasive words of human wisdom." However, it was never about us anyway; it was always about Him.

We can freely admit our own inadequacy, partly because we realize that God's grace becomes more apparent and shines more brightly as a result. If we can keep the focus off of ourselves and on Him, others will see His grace and power in our limitations and weaknesses.

Like Paul, I hope that my readers can look past my own limitations and see that this book is all about Him. It is what He and He only has accomplished that drives the Christian faith and provides the impetus for this book. As Paul wrote later to that same church in Corinth, "But we have this treasure in earthen vessels, that the excellence of the power may be of God and not of us" (2 Corinthians 5:7). He went on to declare,

> And He said to me, 'My grace is sufficient for you, for My strength is made perfect in weakness.' Therefore most gladly I will rather boast in my infirmities, that the power of Christ may rest upon me (2 Corinthians 12:9).

Assumption of Common Ground

There are central, vital elements of the Christian faith with which many or most Bible-believing, God-fearing people already agree. These include the primacy of the cross, as noted above. The Scriptures' emphasis on faith, hope, and love is overwhelming. We may add the importance of worship, fellowship, participation in the local church, and much more.

There is a reason why these crucial topics and themes have not been addressed at length in this book. This apparent omission is not due to the lack of their importance. Rather, I have assumed that these are matters of general consensus. I have addressed instead some of the additions and changes that have occurred throughout church history, matters that have caused or that illustrate the religious divisions in today's world.

Of course, if one were to "get everything right" outwardly, but neglect or minimize mercy, justice, and the love of God, the external things would be of no value. To quote Paul to the Corinthians once again,

> Though I speak with the tongues of men and of angels, but have not love, I have become sounding brass or a clanging cymbal. And though I have the gift of prophecy, and understand all mysteries and all knowledge, and though I have all faith, so that I could remove mountains, but have not love, I am nothing. And though I bestow all my goods to feed the poor, and though I give my body to be burned, but have not love, it profits me nothing (1 Corinthians 13:1–3).

We must always love, keep first things first, and avoid majoring in minors.

Validity of the Restoration Plea

Some readers may question one or more of the specific principles or applications presented in this book. The discussion of matters related to baptism, the Lord's Supper, a cappella singing, and others, may have presented new ideas for some. Some readers may be challenged or even offended by the content or the tone of this material.

One's religious faith is close to one's heart. One may naturally think that what one believes is right, or else one would change. Therefore, it can be extremely hard for one to hear that a cherished religious teaching or practice is false, even if it is because the Bible teaches otherwise. No doubt readers may have found it difficult or painful to consider what has been presented here.

However, in spite of all that the Restoration Plea itself is legitimate. Of course, we may need continual study, understanding, and dialogue regarding specifics. And yet, surely no one can disagree that those who claim and seek to follow Jesus Christ today are seriously divided. The "one body" or church of the New Testament has been threatened and weakened by the multitude of creeds, traditions, and teachings that we see today. How contradictory such division is to Jesus's prayer. He asked the Father,

> I do not pray for these alone, but also for those who will believe in Me through their word; that they all may be one, as You, Father, are in Me, and I in You; that they also may be one in Us, that the world may believe that You sent Me (John 17:20).

It has to be a good thing, a righteous thing, a godly thing, to try to go back to the beginning. It may be messy, difficult, and uncomfortable. We may not get everything perfectly right. We may offend others, though that is not our aim. We may sound like we are promoting "our way" as holier than or superior to others. We may still have a long way to go.

However, regardless of all that, the Restoration Plea is valid. The goal is worthy, and our pursuit of that goal is commendable. So, let's see the "big picture" together and seek to trust and obey just what the Lord gave us at the very beginning.

The Restoration Plea is found in the New Testament itself. At the time of writing of the Revelation, Jesus evaluated seven churches in Asia Minor. He called upon the churches that were no longer faithful to return to Him, to be restored.

For example, in the letter that He had John write to the angel of the church in Ephesus, Jesus said,

> Remember therefore from where you have fallen; repent and do the first works, or else I will come to you quickly and remove your lampstand from its place—unless you repent (Revelation 2:5).

To Sardis He said,

> Remember therefore how you have received and heard; hold fast and repent. Therefore if you will not watch, I will come upon you as a thief, and you will not know what hour I will come upon you (Revelation 3:3).

His inspired words continue to ring true. In our divided religious world today, all professing believers and religious groups must hear what Jesus said to those churches and make application to themselves where appropriate. It is He, not we, who sets the standard on which we must set our aim.

The Basis of Unity

There is a dilemma or conundrum inherent in the Restoration Plea. It has to do with the relationship of unity and truth. In our quest to maintain the unity of the Spirit in the bond of peace (Ephesians 4:3), we dare not forfeit the truth on which that unity is founded. In fact, in that same text in which Paul emphasizes unity, he also writes,

> There is one body and one Spirit, just as you were called in one hope of your calling; one Lord, one faith, one baptism; one God and Father of all, who is above all, and through all, and in you all (Ephesians 4:4–6).

It is very clear that these "ones" are crucial to unity. Disagreement regarding one or more of these "ones" leads to division that is contrary to the will of God.

Some may say, "If you really want to promote unity, you must not insist on doctrinal accuracy. Ignore or overlook those things that separate believers. Don't press too hard on particulars about baptism, worship, or the Lord's Supper. We can all have different views and still be united under one big, diversified tent. Or we can all have our various separate tents on one big, shared campus. That's the only unity that is possible."

Any such proposal to "agree to disagree" regarding clear, biblical teaching, is not only superficial. It obscures the important issues involved and prevents the very discussions and studies that God would have us undertake to accomplish greater unity.

Areas of Opinion

Christians who agree on biblical truths and principles will sometimes differ regarding their applications. Paul and Barnabas publicly disagreed as to whether to include John Mark as a part of their second missionary journey (Acts 15:36–41). Each had a reason for his point of view; neither was wrong from a doctrinal or moral perspective.

When there is a disagreement among Christians, it is wise humbly, and prayerfully to read and study Romans 14 and 1 Corinthians 8 together. Wherever possible, while respecting each person's conscience, explore the basis for each one's opinion. Is there a direct statement from the Bible, a clear example from the Bible, or a necessary implication or inference from the Bible? If so, let each one open the Bible and present his understanding and rationale.

If one cannot convince the other regarding a biblical basis

for his view, let him keep it to himself as a private judgment and not force it on his brother. Let him not insist that the church adhere to his individual conscience, if he lacks a clear scriptural reason for his viewpoint. In all things, let each one treat his brother with love, respect, patience, forbearance, and kindness.

Beyond a Doubt

In many areas of Christian faith and practice, if not most, there is a safe approach that is right and cannot be wrong. There is a solution with which all can agree. For example, there is no dispute that followers of Jesus may biblically be called disciples or Christians. That cannot be wrong! What if we just use such terms found in the Bible and abandon all others, such as denominational names which are non-biblical and divisive?

Here is another. Offering pure vocal praise to God, without mechanical accompaniment, is right and cannot be wrong. There is no question that God accepts congregational singing. Why not leave it that way and avoid the issues that come with adding organs or bands?

What about observing the Lord's Supper on the first day of each week? No one can object biblically to it. It is right and cannot be wrong. To immerse (baptize) a penitent, lost sinner as soon as he or she comes to conviction is clearly established in the Bible. It is right and cannot be wrong. To call the church's leaders elders, overseers, and shepherds (pastors) cannot be wrong.

Paul asked, "For do I now persuade men, or God? Or do I seek to please men? For if I still pleased men, I would not be a bondservant of Christ" (Galatians 1:10). To seek God's favor and not man's, to be simply a bondservant of Christ, that has to be right beyond a doubt!

Questions for Thought and Discussion

1. What did Paul dare to admit about himself and his abilities? Why would he do that?
2. As we pursue fresh waters, can we admit our own inadequacy and limitations? Must we?
3. What are some areas of common ground or consensus, which most religious people affirm?
4. If we restored the church's outward elements, but we lacked love, what would it profit us?
5. "The Restoration Plea is valid, even if our efforts to pursue it are imperfect." Discuss.
6. Where in the New Testament do we hear Jesus calling unfaithful churches to be restored?
7. On what basis must unity be sought, restored, and maintained?
8. Why can sincere religious people not just "agree to disagree" regarding biblical teachings?
9. What two prominent church leaders disagreed in Acts 15:36–41? Over what?
10. What two New Testament chapters will help Christians who have different opinions?
11. How should we approach such differences, respecting each conscience and maintaining unity?
12. What do we mean by "a way that is right and cannot be wrong"?
13. What can happen if all of us sincerely choose simply to seek God's favor and not please man?

Scripture Index

Acknowledgments

I am grateful to Heritage Press for publishing both the first edition and now this revised edition of *Where Fresh Waters Flow: The Restoration Plea*. I especially want to thank my wife, Tanya, for her constant encouragement and support of my efforts. I appreciate Dr. Bill Bagents for writing the foreword and Jamie Cox of the Overton Memorial Library for her assistance throughout the project. In addition, I am indebted to Dr. Batsell Barrett Baxter, Dr. Marlin Connelly, Dr. Harvey Floyd, and other mentors who have impressed upon me the importance of the Restoration Plea. I am dependent on and appreciative of many others whose ideas, teachings, and writings have become ingrained in my own thinking and approach. I am thankful for the elders, deacons, coworkers, and Christian friends who have allowed and encouraged me to preach and teach the Word of God. To God be the glory.

About the Author

Cory Collins is a Bible teacher, preacher, missionary, and author. He and his wife, Tanya, are currently located in Keller, Texas, near Dallas and Fort Worth. Their son Christopher and their daughter Charissa and their families also live in the Dallas area. In the early 1980s, Cory worked in a mission program in Tower One in the World Trade Center in New York City, teaching English and the Bible to immigrants from 25 countries. He has also been involved in missions in Australia, Mexico, Scotland, and South Africa. He was granted his honorary doctorate from Heritage Christian University in 2021. He posts regularly to his blog, "Serving and Sharing."

Also by Cypress Publications

The Christian Life: Chapters for Bible Teachers
by Ed Gallegher

Easing Life's Hurts
by Jack Wilhelm and Bill Bagents

Ecclesiastes: A Document Designed to Disturb
by Coy Roper

Equipping the Saints: A Practical Study of Ephesians 4:11–16
by Bill Bagents and Cory Collins

The Holy Spirit: A Bible Study Guide
by Jack Wilhelm

I AM: A Study of the True and Living God
edited by Jeremy Barrier and Charles R. Webb

Jesus the Christ: Chapters for Bible Teachers
by Ed Gallagher

WHAM! Facing Life's Heavy Hits: Thirteen New Testament Encounters
by Bill Bagents and Laura S. Bagents

WHAM! Facing Life's Heavy Hits: Thirteen Old Testament Encounters
by Bill Bagents and Laura S. Bagents

Wild Transformation
by Matthew Morine

CYPRESS

To see the full catalog of Heritage Christian University Press
and its imprint, Cypress Publications, visit
www.hcu.edu/publications